Combine Scripture, personal experience, and practical application, and you have a powerful message and model of God's multi-ethnic kingdom. This is a *must* for all church leaders who want to truly be the kingdom of God on earth in the second decade of the twenty-first century. Congregations will be transformed taking the journey through Sanders's book!

—Jo Anne Lyon, General Superintendent of The Wesleyan Church

Bridging the Diversity Gap is a must-read for all leaders of churches and Christian organizations who desire to see their ministries reflect the multi-ethnic kingdom God has called us to. Alvin Sanders writes not only theory, but also practical guidance for transforming your ministry. He has mentored me for over five years as we have journeyed together to see the EFCA begin to reflect God's plan for his church.

—William J. Hamel, president of the Evangelical Free Church of America

In our highly racialized society, the church should be leading the way toward reconciliation, modeling before a world torn apart by conflict what it means to love our neighbors as ourselves. Christ has given the church the gift of reconciliation with which to bless the world. Yet it often seems like an uphill battle to build and sustain multi-ethnicity and multicultural understanding within our churches and institutions. Refined and tested in the crucible of real-life leadership, Alvin Sanders has written a positive and practical guide for Christian leaders who are willing to undertake the deeply spiritual work of asset-based diversity development. This book is an invaluable resource that should be required reading for all ministers and lay leaders who are ready (or not) to become intentional about embracing reconciliation as the mission of God in our fallen world.

—Arloa Sutter, executive director of Breakthrough Urban Ministries, Chicago

In *Bridging the Diversity Gap*, Alvin Sanders writes for the church as a practitioner and leader of leaders, lending his down-to-earth style to an otherwise overstuffed subject. As a church planter of an intentionally multi-ethnic church, this book is going to save me many years of headache and mission drift by pushing me beyond popular trends into the deep work of training staff and developing a healthy, multi-ethnic culture throughout the church. Inside are not just the principles for starting new multi-ethnic movements, but also the tools for senior leaders to create change in existing organizations.

—RICH JOHNSON, senior pastor of Sanctuary Columbus Church, Ohio

The term *prophet* is tossed around much too freely today. However, if one defines it as a Christian leader whose experience, wisdom, and heart for God enable that person to communicate complex truths with uncanny clarity, then Alvin Sanders qualifies. *Bridging the Diversity Gap* finds him shedding needed light on the church's call to reflect the values of God's kingdom. It's a challenging call, but you will not find a better teacher and guide than Dr. Sanders.

—EDWARD GILBREATH, journalist and author of *Reconciliation Blues*

Dr. Alvin Sanders's heart bleeds diversity. Like the apostle Paul who gave himself completely to the coming together of Jew and Gentile, Alvin has provided us with the "Pauline nudge" we all need to come out of our ethnic comfort zones, and reach across the divide. This book will be one you will return to again and again as you dream and labor to see your friendships, ministries, and churches reflect our future, diverse, and eternal reality.

—BRYAN LORITTS, lead pastor of Fellowship Memphis
and author of *A Cross Shaped Gospel*

BRIDGING THE DIVERSITY GAP

LEADING TOWARD GOD'S MULTI-ETHNIC KINGDOM

Alvin Sanders

wesleyan
publishing
house

Indianapolis, Indiana

Copyright © 2013 by Alvin Sanders
Published by Wesleyan Publishing House
Indianapolis, Indiana 46250
Printed in the United States of America
ISBN: 978-0-89827-678-7
ISBN (e-book): 978-0-89827-679-4

Library of Congress Cataloging-in-Publication Data

Sanders, Alvin, 1970-
    Bridging the diversity gap : leading toward God's multi-ethnic kingdom / Alvin Sanders.
        pages cm.
    ISBN 978-0-89827-678-7
1. Church and minorities--United States. 2. Race relations--Religious aspects--Christianity.
3. Multiculturalism--Religious aspects--Christianity. I. Title.
    BV4468.S36 2013
    277.3'083089--dc23
                                2013008280

All Scripture quotations, unless otherwise indicated, are taken from the Holy Bible, New International Version®, NIV®. Copyright ©1973, 1978, 1984, by Biblica, Inc. Used by permission of Zondervan. All rights reserved worldwide. www.zondervan.com. The "NIV" and "New International Version" are trademarks registered in the United States Patent and Trademark Office by Biblica, Inc.

Scripture quotations marked (ESV) are from The Holy Bible, English Standard Version® (ESV®), copyright © 2001 by Crossway, a publishing ministry of Good News Publishers. Used by permission. All rights reserved.

All rights reserved. No part of this publication may be reproduced, stored in a retrieval system, or transmitted in any form or by any means—electronic, mechanical, photocopy, recording or any other—except for brief quotations in printed reviews, without the prior written permission of the publisher.

CONTENTS

Foreword   7

Acknowledgements   11

Introduction   13

Part 1. The Challenge of Multi-Ethnicity

  1. Ethnic Borders   33

  2. Racialization   57

  3. Unintentionality   81

Part 2. Shifting toward Multi-Ethnicity

  4. Sustainable Performance   105

  5. Multi-Ethnic Change as Spiritual Growth   131

  6. Changing the Ethnic Game   153

  7. Putting It All Together   171

Learning Lab   187

Case Study   223

Services Available   239

FOREWORD

When I was ten years old, my brother, our friends, and I dreamed of building a fort. It would be our hideout, our place to have meetings and hang out, and, of course, a place where no girls were allowed. To our ten-year-old minds, nothing at the time could be as cool as having our own fort. We often discussed what it would look like, how big it would be, and what would go in it. We talked about it for a long time, but that is all we did—talk about it. Our problem was that no one actually knew how to build a fort or where we would get the money and materials to build it. Though we longed for our own fort, no one knew enough to effectively lead us in building it.

That is, until the day when my father overheard my brother and me dreaming about our fort. Recalling his own boyhood dreams of having a fort, he began to teach us what we needed to know—the basic principles of building, how to design the fort, how to find building materials for free at dump sites, how to use the tools he had, and how to divide the work among the boys so we could actually build the fort.

Armed with this incredible gift of knowledge and principles for designing, building, and organizing, my brother and I set out to finally make the often-dreamed-of fort a reality. We met with our friends to tell them it could really happen and talk about the steps we needed to take. We drew up plans, and we arranged for our dads to drive us to dump sites so we could collect crates, wood, and other building materials. We selected a site, and we arranged "work" schedules to build the fort.

And build it we did. It took a few months, but when it was completed, it was even more than we originally hoped for. It had windows with shutters, a round door, an eight-foot ceiling with a loft, cable spools for tables, a comfy sofa, bean bag chairs, shag carpeting, and even a light so we could stay in to the wee hours of the night watching *Monday Night Football* on a little black-and-white TV. The fort became the ultimate place for the boys of the neighborhood to hang out, listen to a transistor radio, talk, laugh, and camp out. It helped form many friendships and memories.

Looking back at that time with fondness, I am reminded that it only happened because my father took the time to teach my brother and me the necessary principles to lead our friends in constructing the fort. He gave us the knowledge we needed and the practical know-how to achieve our dream.

Such is the book *Bridging the Diversity Gap*. Many of us have, for some time now, dreamed of a church that is diverse and unified within its congregations. To that end, we have a growing number of books on diversity in the church, reconciliation, and the theology of unity. What we lack is a book that focuses on leadership. Without effective leaders, all the books in the world about God's heart for reconciliation and the fullness of his diverse church will simply gather dust or sit on hard drives, resting as forgotten files. They will be unrealized dreams.

We need focused action motivated by leaders and led by God. Alvin Sanders has been leading in these areas for many years, and he brings his wisdom to the writing of *Bridging the Diversity Gap*. And what a gift this book is! Combining his rigorous understanding of Scripture with hard-earned experience often forged in the combination of failure and victory, we now have a book leaders can turn to for tried-and-true principles.

What is so refreshing about this book is that it does not try to Christianize secular diversity principles. In fact, as you will see from the start, *Bridging the Diversity Gap* argues that such an approach cannot work. Rather, given the important organizational differences between Christian organizations and secular ones, we must begin with Christian principles that can be applied to the diversity work at hand. Put another way, rather than attempting to use a shovel to mortar our bricks together, we must learn to use a trowel with powerful new results.

I liken Alvin Sanders's work in this book to the work my father did for my brother and me. My dad unleashed the ability to build the fort we craved, and in *Bridging the Diversity Gap*, Alvin Sanders unleashes the ability of Christian leaders to build the diverse, unified, reconciled church we—and God—crave. This book is a true gift that will have substantial, long-lasting impact.

—MICHAEL O. EMERSON
professor at Rice University and author of *Divided by Faith*, *United by Faith*, *Transcending Racial Barriers*, and *People of the Dream*

ACKNOWLEDGEMENTS

To my wife, Caroline, thanks for your love and support of my ministry. To my kids, Hannah and Gabby, thanks for sharing me with the ministry world. To the "original" Alvin Sanders (my dad) and my uncle, Cleve, thanks for teaching me how to work and for your life guidance over the years. To my mother, Jessie, thanks for introducing me to Christ and for your unwavering support. To the "Moses generation" of River of Life who served alongside me and Caroline from 2000–2007, your sacrifice will never be forgotten on earth or in heaven. To Jon Weatherly, David Faust, Roger Howell, and the Directional Team of the Evangelical Free Church of America (ECFA), thanks for believing and investing in me.

To all my colleagues at the EFCA, your sage wisdom, endless support, and willingness to put up with my flaws have made ministry a privilege. It is an honor to serve with you.

INTRODUCTION

First things first—I am not a guru. My aim is to offer you a practical leadership process to lead your organization toward multi-ethnicity. Feel free to adapt the philosophy and process I am about to unpack to fit your particular situation. I've intentionally written this in a casual manner because so many books on this topic are written in a technical or academic style. I want it to seem like you are interacting with me in one of my presentations.

Basically, this is my story of what has worked for me. Hopefully, it will work for you. I want to be your guide, helping you take your good intentions and lead your organization across the ethnic divide. I know many are out there who desire this, because over the years I have met hundreds of you. Many are frustrated because they can't seem to get permanent traction toward ethnic change within their organizations.

Every year I have the privilege of attending a pastoral learning community facilitated by Larry Osborne, who serves as teaching pastor of North Coast Community Church in Vista, California. It is one of the most dynamic learning atmospheres I have ever been in. Larry is the author of several books, most notably one entitled *Sticky Church*.[1] In the book, he makes the case that closing the back door of your church is even more important than opening the front door wider, and he offers a time-tested, proven strategy for doing so. Pastors, regardless of race, social class, and denomination love this book.

Years of attending those meetings and reflecting on *Sticky Church* are the genesis of this book. I wondered what would a *Sticky Church* "type" book look like that put forth easy-to-follow principles for Christian leaders of churches, nonprofits, and universities who desired to make multi-ethnicity "sticky"?

From my experience, there are three types of reasons why an organization feels compelled to pursue multi-ethnicity—financial, legal, or moral. Of course, there can be combinations of these, but one of them always seems to rise to the top as the foundational motivation.

The foundational motivation is extremely important because it sets the course for the rest of the programming. When it comes to this topic, one cannot take some secular diversity program, sprinkle it with a couple of Scriptures, and expect it to have a strong impact.

I know this because I have been involved in secular diversity training. Sure, we can learn from those programs, but they don't meet the needs of our distinctively Christian situations. The philosophy that undergirds them is not designed for our organizations. The organizational culture is vastly different in the Christian context from secular institutions.

By organizational culture, I'm referring to the pattern of development reflected in our policies (courses of action), practices (habits and customs), and procedures (day-to-day rituals). Secular and Christian organizations share some similarities, but there are fundamental differences that make them district from one another.

If you work for a corporation, your bottom line is to make money. Christian organizations are typically nonprofits, so profits are not (or should not be) the main goal. Christian organizations are also unique in the nonprofit world, because they adhere to biblically based ethics. The combination of being both Christian and nonprofit means that these organizational cultures typically have dynamics that others don't.

For instance, I highly doubt Coca-Cola opens its board meetings with an extended time of prayer. In Christian organizations, people who work there have a heightened sense of ownership. After all, it is not just a place of employment, but an extension of their faith. In fact, many have left much-higher-paying jobs in order to work in Christian environments. So things like faith, tradition, legacy, and shared governance hold much more sway in this context than the typical secular corporation or nonprofit.

The distinctive DNA of Christian organizations often unintentionally results in a stubborn culture that is slow and resistant to change of any type, let alone change with the potential to be divisive like racial diversity. To be successful, Christian organizations need to be, as Matthew 10:16 states, "wise as serpents and innocent as doves" (ESV).

Here is the dirty little secret about the majority of those who have decision-making power within Christian organizations: Their time mainly consists of juggling three types of resources—people, money, and facilities. They work tirelessly to put a lot of people in the pews of churches, the seats of colleges, and in the programming of nonprofit ministries. They have highly orchestrated financial campaigns to erect beautiful buildings for ministry service. They work those budgets, making money stretch.

Don't worry, as I am not about to lay a guilt trip on you about this leadership reality. What I will warn is to be careful about letting this be your only measuring stick as a leader. The need to focus on balancing people, money, and facilities can potentially create a huge tension for leaders interested in ethnic integration. Many of the constituents these leaders represent or work for really don't understand the need for the organization to pursue diversity. Constituents may think resources and energy should be invested in "more important" matters.

There is only one sufficient answer to those who question the motives of these leaders: Multi-ethnicity is a mark of the gospel. Those other things are measured because they can indicate one kind of *success*. However, there is also the kingdom *significance* of both one's leadership and the institutions being led.

The balance leaders have to strike is to be successful at managing people, money, and facilities, while keeping organizations significant for the sake of the kingdom. Many organizations have large numbers of employees, huge budgets, and beautiful buildings but are not significant to the mission field they are set up to serve. I know of one historically Christian college that the ethnically diverse residents of the surrounding neighborhood call "the plantation" with good reason. God cannot be pleased about that.

KINGDOM PRIORITIES

Significance comes through one thing: chasing kingdom priorities. We as Christian leaders have a unique role in this world. We are charged to lead the citizens of the kingdom of God. If we are smart, we follow the example of Christ, mentoring those for whom we are responsible in the values, attitudes, and beliefs of the kingdom. We often see Jesus testing the motives of people who followed him by challenging their priorities. His curriculum for his followers was modeling and teaching them characteristics of the kingdom.

One well-known example can be found in Luke 10:25–37, the parable of the good Samaritan. In this passage, an expert in the Hebrew law asked Jesus what he had to do to inherit eternal life. Jesus answered by asking him what was written in the Law. The expert quoted Deuteronomy 6:5 and Leviticus 19:18—to love God with all one's heart, soul, and mind. Jesus commended him for his answer.

But in Luke 10:29, we see a tension developing between kingdom significance and the world's definition of success. The expert wanted to clarify whether it was enough to successfully keep the command-ment according to his ethnic group's definition of *neighbor* (only loving other Jews). So Jesus told the famous Good Samaritan story. Understand that in their world, Jews and Samaritans were heated ethnic rivals. They would have had no love for each other.

Imagine that while driving from St. Louis to Kansas City, I crash my car into a ditch. Some black pastors from thriving ministries see me (I'm black) in obvious pain but decide to keep driving. Then the Grand Dragon of the Ku Klux Klan pulls up to me. He tears his white hood to make a bandage for my wounds. He then pulls out some medicine from his first-aid kit from the trunk, applies it, and then calls 9-1-1. He trails the ambulance I'm in to the nearest hospital and tells the admitting nurse to bill him for any expenses incurred for my care.

By now you may be smirking, because it is very unlikely for that to happen; and that's the point of the parable of the good Samaritan—kingdom transcendence (right belief plus right action) over worldly ethnic boundaries. By telling this story, Jesus was emphasizing that loving God will cause a radical transformation of how you treat people, especially those who are ethnically different from you. He was saying that if you truly love God, you will demonstrate that love by loving your neighbors just like the Samaritan loved the Jew in need. It was a lesson on kingdom significance versus worldly success.

It is important to note that the parable of the good Samaritan was considered to be a recounting of a true story that was commonly known to the audience Christ was addressing. It would be like mentioning 9/11 in the United States. Those of us who were around during that tragedy immediately have a common reference point. Jesus was giving them a literal, real-life example of what the kingdom looked like. Right belief *must* be married to right actions. Otherwise what you believe will be rendered powerless (Luke 10:36–37).

Another example of earthly success versus kingdom significance can be found in Matthew 15:21–28. Here we find an ethnically Canaanite woman, who at that time would typically be considered an enemy of Israel. She asked Jesus to cast demons from her daughter. No doubt her ethnicity, gender, and pagan standing played a role in the disciples, urging Jesus to "send her away, for she keeps crying out after us" (Matt. 15:23). To achieve success in the ancient Jewish context, one didn't intermingle with her kind. No one cared about her needs; she was simply an inconvenience.

At first Jesus' response in Matthew 15:24 seems to be denying her request, seemingly calling her a dog in verse 26. (To be called a dog was an insult then as it is now.) But it soon became obvious that Jesus was not insulting the woman, but rather manipulating the situation to teach his disciples about the kingdom. They didn't think this woman was worth bothering with, mainly because of their prejudice toward her. In the end, Jesus not only granted her request, but also praised her for her faith (v. 28). His message was clear: prejudice and ethnocentrism are opposed to the kingdom.

A kingdom priority like multi-ethnicity is measured by the sincere work we do. Multi-ethnicity is a value that Jesus and the early church passionately pursued. Pursing a multi-ethnic vision may or may not enhance success in the world's eyes, but it will please the Lord. So here's a question for you to ponder: Is that enough?

MY JOURNEY

The book of Lamentations might not be on the top of your reading list, but its lessons need to be heeded. The essence of the book can be found in Lamentations 1:16: "No one is near to comfort me, no one to restore my spirit."

Lament is a part of leadership throughout Scripture. Moses, Esther, Jesus, and many more practiced lament. Lament wrestles with the tension between earthly reality and kingdom pursuit. To lament is to admit we don't have all the answers. It is the art of deep disappointment. I'm not talking about disappointment because your favorite sports team lost or because it rained most of the time during your vacation. I'm talking about the life situations that, if not dealt with, will lead to despair. Deep disappointment can be lethal to leadership, or it can be an opportunity to mature. By navigating lament, you can transform difference from a barrier into an opportunity. Learning to navigate lament defines my journey.

In April 2001, Timothy Thomas, a nineteen-year-old African-American with a history of nonviolent misdemeanors, was shot and killed by a Cincinnati police officer. His death caused outrage in the neighborhood of my then multi-ethnic church plant (River of Life), resulting in millions of dollars of damage due to rioting.

It was in this environment that we at River of Life started ministry in the very neighborhood that had been at the center of the rioting. River of Life became a tangible demonstration of what God can do when people from all walks of life live in unity for the advancement of the kingdom.

For seven years as the founding pastor, I was surrounded by the effects of ethnic conflict. In leading that wonderful ministry, I learned that *multi-ethnicity* is a verb and is much bigger than merely achieving harmony. I have come to believe that it is a bridge to fulfilling the Great Commission, which is impossible without following the first and second Great Commandments: love God and love your neighbor as yourself (Matt. 22:37–40).

When I pastored River of Life, 70 percent of those who joined were unchurched. Most told me one of the big reasons they came was the fact that everybody was accepted there, regardless of their cultural background. That is the heroic, happy ending. But to get to that point, I had to learn the skill of navigating lament.

The leadership journey always begins within. It is difficult to lead anybody anywhere we haven't been ourselves. At the core, leading toward God's multi-ethnic kingdom is an expression of God's work within us. The world is broken, and one of the results is division along racial lines. How broken is your heart over this? More importantly, are you willing to lead others to do something about it? Is healing this rift an organizational hill you are willing to "die" on?

Three years into the planting of River of Life, things were going extremely well. We started with my family and had grown quickly. Through the wonderful generosity of our parent church, we obtained an old hardware store to renovate. Through the gifts of foundations and Christian business professionals, 350,000 dollars had been raised toward renovation. People. Money. Facilities. We were on our way to success.

Or so I thought. In a six-month period, we lost 35 percent of our people. I began to do exit interviews and could not believe my ears as to the reasons people left. They revealed a pattern of tension that indicated I had not done a good job of leading kingdom transcendence. "We don't believe the races should worship together; I don't want my kids involved with poor kids; black people are too loud; your wife shouldn't be on stage opening the service because a man should do it." Those exit interviews pretty much destroyed my paradigm of success.

I was in a place of despair. Here were people in whom I had invested for years, yet they had bailed on me and the multi-ethnic vision. To be honest, my spirit was weak, my will failing, and I was ready to resign. But before I did, I decided to fast and seek the Lord's wisdom.

After I emerged, it was clear that God was not calling me to quit; he was calling me to focus on chasing the kingdom. Regardless of the response of the people, my job was to call them to truth and righteousness. Those years I spent shepherding a multi-ethnic church in the midst of an ethnically conflicted community have made me the Christ follower I am today.

My time as pastor of River of Life is the foundational part of my story. Another chapter is my stint as director of ethnic ministry at Cincinnati Christian University. I owe the people there a great debt. They allowed me to develop new theories of what to do, and then test-drive the ideas on the campus.

Some things I implemented soared with the eagles, and other programs crashed like the *Titanic*. However, overall there was great fruit. Among the highlights were ethnically integrating full-time faculty for the first time in school history, and making tremendous strides toward integrating the student body.

The present chapter of my journey is serving in senior leadership for the Evangelical Free Church of America (EFCA). We continue to work toward reaching our goal to multiply transformational churches among all ethnic people both nationally and globally.

I share these snapshots of my journey for your assurance. What you are about to read was born primarily through my passion for God's multi-ethnic kingdom, on-the-job training, and time spent in the "ivory tower" of academia. I have worked extensively on this topic in the very real settings of a church and university and within a denomination. I have earned a PhD studying this topic, and I also serve as an adjunct professor at several seminaries. So be assured that what you are about to read has been tested.

SOME PRELIMINARY CONSIDERATIONS

Let me list the biases of this book. The focus is narrow and only on ethnic diversity. Many people say, "But what about social class, gender, disability, age, etc.?" Within my organization, I actively work to address them, and I encourage everyone reading this book to engage those other areas of diversity. I have chosen to specifically focus only on ethnicity within this work, which is my main area of expertise. Please don't misinterpret my narrow focus as somehow degrading the other forms of diversity. They are extremely important.

Another bias to be aware of is that the majority of my examples come from a black/white paradigm. I talk about other ethnicities, but my illustrations are skewed for a simple reason: I draw mostly from my life experience, which stems from being black and serving in majority white organizations. Although this is the case, the points made still hold for other cross-ethnic relations. I ask that this bias not be misinterpreted to mean other racial dynamics are not important.

The last bias to be aware of is that this book is aimed at majority-white, Christian organizations that desire to ethnically integrate and are either near the beginning of the process or have tried and failed. If your organization is further down the road, this will be helpful as well, but my assumption is novice level. Racially speaking, it's not that things can't go the other way. I believe there is a whole other set of issues if we are talking about, say, a majority African-American, Asian, or Latino organization that desires to become whiter. But I believe that would require somewhat different strategies.

What I am looking to do is give general insight and general solutions for your specific situation. We are cruising at thirty thousand feet, not at the grassroots. How your specific challenges and solutions (in relation to the insight I am giving) play out is up to you. Actually, it is not totally up to you; it's up to you, your decision-makers, and the Holy Spirit.

Fight against your natural inclination to read this book alone and then act like Moses, descending from the mountain to lay out edicts for the people to follow. I know from both my personal experience and the many lessons I have learned from others that type of leadership style will not work when leading a transition to multi-ethnicity. The way to go is to harness the power of Christian leadership communities.

A Christian leadership community is a group of people who form their lives together to work toward leading kingdom citizens. Examples are a Christian university board, church (or nonprofit) ministry team, or denominational staff. These communities operate as spaces where people reflect on their life experiences. As they reflect, others offer varying viewpoints, allowing people to unearth common understanding as well as differences.

Knowledge construction in the midst of relationship is part of what binds us together as leaders. Therefore, you would be doing yourself and the organization you lead a great disservice to read this alone. You need a community of learners to process ideas. So if you are a senior pastor, read this with your staff. If you serve in nonprofit or university leadership, read it with your board and other decision-makers. Make sure to intentionally set aside times to discuss the concepts presented. I recommend taking your time, reading a chapters and then processing the questions in the learning lab (at the end of this book) after each reading.

OVERVIEW OF THE BOOK

I recommend you read the chapters in order. Many of you are like me in believing that when you buy a book, you can scan and skip around, reading the parts you think are relevant to your situation. If you choose to go that route with this book, you will miss some key insights. The content flow is intermingled, each chapter building upon the previous one. You may not understand the reasoning of the later chapters if you haven't read the previous ones.

In part 1, I will describe the three challenges we all face with ethnic diversity. The first is rooted in ethnic borders (chapter 1). Ethnic borders are those cultural traits we tightly hold on to that define our ethnic identity. Most ethnic folk are aware of theirs while most whites are not. Most people, regardless of ethnicity, are typically not very flexible in moving the borders. Unearthing and negotiating these is half the battle.

The second challenge is racialization (chapter 2). "A racialized society is a society wherein race matters profoundly for differences in life experiences, life opportunities, and social relationships. . . . [It is one] that allocates different economic, political, social, and even psychological rewards to groups along racial lines."[2] Racialization is why color blindness is not the answer.

The third challenge is unintentionality (chapter 3). Most Christian organizations did not have multi-ethnic in mind when they started. Besides not having multi-ethnic in mind, the Christian traditions from which our institutions sprung are not all the same. We all possess what I call "founding DNA." Our efforts must be connected with this.

Will describe how to begin shifting your church, Christian college, or Christian nonprofit organization toward multi-ethnicity.

We begin to discuss why transitioning to multi-ethnicity is a very complex task (chapter 4). In fact, it may be unlike anything you have attempted to lead before. The leadership required is highly situational and contingent. It is more of an art than a science. I call the type of leadership you need to use "asset-based diversity development," which is a philosophy that guides you to lead not from a base of deficiencies and needs caused by the three challenges, but instead to leverage differences by unlocking your organization's capacities and gifts. This serves as your diversity bridge by creating a ripple effect. It requires making some basic shifts in thinking. Chapters 5 to 7 are about these shifts.

The first shift is from secular to spiritual (chapter 5). Theories of secular diversity are helpful and informative. However, they lack kingdom power and transcendence. They should never serve as the foundation for Christian integration efforts, but as supplements.

Multi-ethnicity efforts based on secularized notions of diversity have little spiritual impact because their foundation is humanitarianism, not Scripture. Our number one asset is the Bible.

The second shift is from tweaking to transformative leadership (chapter 6). Getting to multi-ethnicity is not something where you can tweak a few things and move on. Tweaking is fear-based change. We are afraid to significantly rock the boat, so we hope we can tweak our way out of our predicaments. It never works.

The last shift is from accidental to accountability and alignment (chapter 7). What else is needed to turn your good intentions into good fruit? Your followers need boundaries because boundaries give clarity. If it is fuzzy to you, it will be a fog to the people you lead. People need to be pointed in the right direction and then held accountable. To do so will require leadership providing a basic framework to operate in.

The framework creates the asset of multi-ethnic clarity, providing the vision for the unified effort we all desire. No matter how good your intentions are, it is going to be hard to build multi-ethnic into your DNA unless you create a compass to guide people over the gap. If you don't develop one, you are guaranteed to create confusion, disappointment, and racial fatigue.

This book also includes a learning lab and a case study that will help you implement asset-based diversity development in your church or organization.

Don't expect to find all the answers in this book. I'm just passing along the lessons the Lord has taught me with the hope of blessing you. Hopefully, this is one of many steps on your journey. When a leadership team loves and pursues multi-ethnicity, the people start to understand and embrace it. If you are willing to boldly lead a team down this road, it will be one of the most satisfying spiritual walks you will ever experience.

NOTES

1. Larry Osborne, *Sticky Church* (Grand Rapids, Mich.: Zondervan, 2008).

2. Michael O. Emerson and Christian Smith, *Divided by Faith: Evangelical Religion and the Problem of Race in America* (Oxford: Oxford University Press, 2000), 7.

THE CHALLENGE PART ONE
OF MULTI-ETHNICITY

ETHNIC BORDERS

There are over seven hundred references to ethnic groups in Scripture. Seeing color is not ungodly. And the Bible does not ask us to give up our ethnicity or to replace it with some generic notion of nonethnic Christianity. After all, Jesus embraced his ethnicity.

Ethnic borders are cultural traits that define our ethnic identity for ourselves and others. Today, Christians are one in Christ, but our ethnic differences do not pass away with salvation. Christ's goal was not to eliminate ethnicity but to transcend it.

Organizations that accept ethnicity as a normal part of the human experience will acknowledge, appreciate, and leverage differences instead of denigrating or ignoring them. These organizations would be following in the footsteps of our biblical forebearers.

FAMILY FEUD

So let's start with some theological reflection, beginning with the real-world perspective of the biblical story. One way to view the Bible is as a narrative that intends to reframe reality through the lens of God. Readers are challenged to submit to the reality presented in Scripture, love the God who is represented, and obey his commands.

To understand our response to racialization from a biblical point of view, we must see how God's desire for unity operates throughout Scripture—from the very beginning, through the ebb and flow of sin and division, to the end. We must see how interrupting processes such as racialization is *God's* idea.

One Family Divided

Think of people groups as one giant family—large, colorful, diverse . . . and dysfunctional! The Bible depicts a world of smaller, competing families known as nations. The links that form these families—whose members share familiar origins and basics of culture, such as language, values, attitudes, and beliefs—we label as ethnic.

Throughout the biblical record, we see a theme of struggle, discrimination, and conflict: one story after another of individuals and ethnic groups trying to advance their own interests over others. It is a sure recipe for division rather than unity.

If we are not careful, as we follow the biblical story, we might mistakenly think people ethnically different from Israel are "the enemy." Yet in reality, we face an army of evil spiritual beings whose goal is to frustrate God's efforts toward a united, inclusive family in Christ (Eph. 6:12).

When we watch the news and see stories of "ethnic cleansing" or when we look at a history book and see the abuses people groups suffered because of their race, we cannot forget that the root of these events is spiritual. Therefore, the primary way to address these and other evil atrocities should be rooted in spiritual practice.

When it comes to reconciliation, the first step of the church in a deeply broken world is not strategy, but prayer. Cardinal Joseph Bernardin wrote in *The Gift of Peace* that prayer is closing "the gap between what [we are] and what God wants of [us]."[1] We will not be successful unless we develop a vibrant, strong prayer life to close the gap.

The gap exists because, as sinners, we are all in some degree of rebellion against God. Psalm 2:1 asks, "Why do the nations conspire and the peoples plot in vain?" The quick answer is because they are in rebellion. Let's now take a look at the root of the rebellion.

The Unraveling of Shalom

In Genesis 2, we see God's plan for unity in the garden of Eden. Relationships were perfect between people and God, between people themselves, and with the environment. It was truly a blessed state of existence. Actually, the word *blessed* does not accurately describe what was going on. A better word is a Hebrew one, *shalom*, meaning people living in a situation of completeness in every aspect of their human existence.

Take a moment and think of every single need that you and the world around you have. After compiling your list, imagine if they all were completely fulfilled. That's *shalom*. In the garden of Eden, Adam and Eve experienced it. Their physical, social, moral, mental, and emotional needs were completely met. And their spiritual relationship with God was without filters — 100 percent pure. Theirs was a life with no worries.

Then the familiar story of Genesis 3 tells of the moment when the whole situation of *shalom* unraveled, beginning the dysfunctional mess of a family we have today. By *mess* I mean the change that occurs in the personal character of humans, brought about by the willful disobedience of Adam and Eve. With their sin, God's original intent for our world — to live in unity with each other and with him — was violated.

The consequences of the fall were instant: Confidence was replaced by doubt; honesty was replaced by deception; intimacy was replaced by shame; fellowship was replaced by fear. Barriers went up between Adam and Eve and between both them and God. And along with the barriers came hostility.

God questioned Adam; Adam blamed Eve; and Eve blamed the snake. Adam and Eve showed the first signs of human conflict and rebellion against God, a rebellion that continues to have far-reaching effects. In Genesis 3:15, God spoke to the evil being (represented by the serpent) that started it all: "And I will put enmity between you and the woman, and between your offspring and hers; he will crush your head, and you will strike his heel."

This verse foretells how our world will be in continual conflict between humans and representatives of evil. The battle lines have been formed, and the world from now until Christ's return will struggle in a messy conflict. The apostle Paul called the time between the fall and Christ's return "the present evil age" (Gal. 1:4). Traditionally, Genesis 3:15 has been interpreted as a foreshadowing of Christ's eventual defeat of Satan. We know that Christ came to reconcile people to their God, to each other, and to creation.

Reconciliation

Let's now reflect on how Christ entered the world. A good place to start is with Abraham and Sarah. In Genesis 12:2–3, God promised them, "I will make you into a great nation and I will bless you; I will make your name great, and you will be a blessing. I will bless those who bless you, and whoever curses you I will curse; and all peoples on earth will be blessed through you."

See once again God's desire for unity: a unified nation, bringing blessing to all. Yet to receive the promise of God, Abraham had to make a couple of choices: to stay in his homeland or go to a new one, and to stay with his biological family and promised inheritance or to leave to start a new family with his (infertile) wife. All the choices boiled down to whether Abraham was going to trust God and obey the call on his life. He had to act in faith. Abraham left behind more than family and comfort when he chose to follow God; he also left behind ethnic tradition. Let me explain.

In the ancient world, it was thought that gods were bound by certain criteria, one of which was that a god could not cross ethnic borders. The god of Ur and the Chaldeans could not be the god of, say, Egypt and the Egyptians. In other words, gods were segregated by ethnic enclaves.

The God of the Hebrews was challenging Abraham to break out of that belief system, declaring that he was the type of God who could travel anywhere and be over any people group. By agreeing to move, Abraham was agreeing to convert to an entirely different tradition. He truly was exhibiting tremendous faith.

In Genesis 15, God brought even more clarity to his plan for using Abraham and Sarah to restore unity. He declared that they would have a son, and their offspring would fulfill the promise of blessing all the people of the world. And in Genesis 26:4, God reminded Abraham's son Isaac of that promise. Then, in Genesis 28:4, he reminded Isaac's son Jacob of the promise as well. The existence of a genealogy was in itself a confirmation of the promise.

The tangible blessing did not come overnight. After Genesis, the story expanded beyond individuals to the complete sum of Abraham's offspring, which eventually became known as the nation of Israel.

In Exodus we see the pitting of nation against nation as a contest between gods. For example, the famous plagues of Exodus 1–12 were each a "contest" between the God of Israel and one of Egypt's false gods. When God rescued the Israelites, he delivered the message that the God of Israel is the sovereign God over all, regardless of ethnicity. As more and more non-Israelites recognized this, they switched allegiances.

Consider Joshua 2 and the story of Rahab; read the story of Naomi and Ruth in the book of Ruth; ponder God's message to the Israelite captives in Babylon found in Jeremiah 29:4–7. Throughout the Old Testament, the message to the Israelites was clear that he was a God of ethnic inclusion.

The Witness of God's People

We see from this brief look at the Old Testament that the main avenue God used to reveal himself was the witness of his people— Abraham's biological descendants, the nation of Israel. People who wanted to know God often found him through Israelites. In the New Testament, the witness was expanded. A mystery was revealed.

The apostle Paul reminded the Galatians that they began their relationship with God the same way Abraham had: by faith (Gal. 3:6–9). Abraham's real offspring are those who have faith in his God, not his ethnic descendants. The redemption of Christ permits *all* to enjoy the blessing of Abraham (Gal. 3:14). No longer did people need to seek out Israelites and convert to Judaism. That was the old paradigm. We are now told to receive the promise of the Spirit and form communities of Spirit-filled people. These ministry communities are the primary vehicles for the nations to know God.

The stress of the New Testament is toward a community of people making their presence known by living differently as the people of God in their geographic region. As they do this, the people of their region will know where to look for God.

You can find examples of these ethical encouragements in each of Paul's epistles. These instructions of how to live the Christian life are not geared toward individuals, but rather toward the community of believers. The concern is with the character of the church, stressing how the people of God should live in a rebellious, conflicted world. This is no small concern, as nothing less than the essence of the gospel is at stake.

Jesus set a clear pattern concerning how the gospel was going to spread: people influencing others to follow Jesus through the witness of their lives. First there were twelve (John 1:35–50); then seventy-two (Luke 10:1); then at least one hundred twenty (Acts 1:15); then more than three thousand (Acts 2:41); then millions, all through the simple concept of Spirit-filled communities living differently from the world around them. We are citizens of the kingdom of God, a holy nation that acts as ambassadors of reconciliation to a conflicted world in rebellion (2 Cor. 5:11–21).

In a reunited family, value and significance don't lie in race, ethnicity, power, wealth, gender, or any other attitude found in the rebellious world. In the reunited family called the church, our values, attitudes, and beliefs have been radically restructured through the power of the Holy Spirit (Gal. 3:26–29). The source of this reunited family is none other than God.

We are told in 2 Corinthians 5:18 that God gave the church the gift of reconciliation. In a world where conflict reigns supreme, only God can cause a family reunion of all people. It is God's initiative and his work. The reunited family called the church becomes a witness to a world marred by conflict.

PERSONAL IDENTITY

As we see in Scripture, ethnicity plays a huge role in defining identity. When speaking of identity, I'm using the concept in the sense that it is the way we present who we are to others as well as ourselves. When constructing a sense of identity, we have to recognize that we are always partly unique and partly a creation of our society. These two aspects can never be isolated from each other.

This is contrarian thinking for all of us who grew up in an extremely individualistic society like the United States. We possess a strong belief about the uniqueness of the individual, which sociologists call individualism. We tend toward placing individual choice at the zenith of how we view things. We are predisposed to thinking we are independent of everything when we form ideas about who we are.

So common thought is that we assume we can separate from societal connections and rationally think through situations independent of outside influencers (like race). But this is not the case. The thoughts we claim as independently unique to us are still dependent on where we learned what particular things mean, which is heavily influenced by the society we live in.

Saying we are always partly unique and partly a creation of society doesn't mean we have no individual uniqueness or that we can't possess a theology that embraces absolute truth. We obviously have a choice to form our own personal identities. But our unique self is shaped both by our society and our unique choices.

Three Parts of Our Identity

As Christians we can think of ourselves as having three overlapping parts. The first part is what we often stress the most, which is our biblical self. Our chief identity is in Christ, and we spend our lives studying his teachings and trying to live them out the best way we know how.

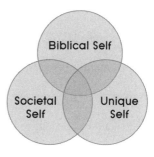

The second part is our societal self. This is how we are identified by society. We all possess many labels. For example, I am labeled black, male, Christian, middle class, tall, etc. The list is endless. Each one of the labels assigned to me carries a certain connotation in the society in which I live. And I have no control over it. Some labels I reject and some I accept, but all have an influence in forming me.

What we do have complete control over is the third part, which is our unique self. We personally associate a certain amount of importance to each label that has been given to us from society. I determine how important race, gender, social class, and other social labels are in my life.

Here is the mistake people often make. We focus so intensely only on our biblical selves, and it's not the full reality. You're biblical, societal, and unique selves are constantly informing one another, because they are intertwined. They are not fixed, but flexible, always evolving, and influenced by life experience. The person you were at twenty-three years old is not the same as the person you are at fifty-three. Through this constant interaction, you form your personal identity.

For example, in certain ethnic communities, conversations about personal identity are very overt and active. A lot of times the conversations revolve around how much "whiteness" is allowable. Typically, from the white perspective, most haven't thought deeply about what it means to be white in America. The ethnic identity we possess, like it or not, positions us in the whole racialization process, which I will talk about in the next chapter.

Why Identity Matters

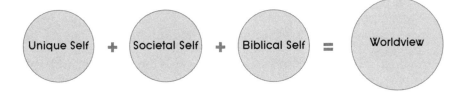

Unique Self **+** Societal Self **+** Biblical Self **=** Worldview

Consider this analogy as an explanation of why this matters in leading multi-ethnic organizations.

Occasionally, I receive free tickets to a sporting event. Sometimes I get cheap seats in the upper deck, from where the participants look like ants; more often though, I get tickets for great seats. When you sit in great seats, the action is so vivid and intense, the amenities are great, and you feel that you are part of the game. What if I gave you those tickets? And what if after the game, you did a little experiment?

You asked ten different people sitting in totally different parts of the stadium, "What happened?" You know what you would get? Ten answers containing both similarities and differences. In fact, even though each person was watching the same game in the same stadium, you might not be able to tell that based on the variety of responses. How you view the game is *totally* dependent on your seat location. People in the great seats would have a different perspective from those who sit in the cheap seats, even though they saw the same game in the same stadium.

Now imagine you have tickets to the game of life. If you think of life as a game being played in a stadium, then your personal identity (made up of societal, biblical, and unique selves) is your seat in the stadium. Everyone in the stadium can see the action, but no one sees it exactly the same. They have only the perspective from their seat. We label our seat location as our worldview. That is the practical implication we must pay attention to as leaders.

The Twin Forces

Missions historian Andrew Walls uses the phrase the "twin forces of Christian history" to describe an indigenizing principle and a pilgrim principle.[2] The indigenizing principle says there is no such thing as a Christian who is not heavily influenced by the society to which he or she belongs. Applying this principle to our three selves means that we must reconcile the gospel with our societal selves in order for us to accept Christ in our unique selves, creating our biblical selves. Combine the three and we have our worldview. This is why spreading the gospel is easier in certain situations than in others.

If a society revolves around Islam, it is going to be much harder to convince people there is another way to God. This is because we are somewhat a prisoner to our society and need to be liberated from many aspects of it. Walls describes this liberating force as the pilgrim principle. This principle requires us to change some societal values to which we are bound to match up with biblical teachings. The older saints at the church I grew up in used to call this principle being in the world but not of it. In seminary they called it sanctification. It's the process of eliminating those things from our lives that are sinful. For our purposes, it's moving from an ethnocentric perspective to a Christ-centered one.

Based on our personal identities, we all come to the table with ethnic values. When we talk about these values, we are talking about whether we consider something right or wrong based on our ethnic heritages. These values help us determine what we consider to be normal. We all have these rules of behavior—often learned innately rather than taught—and if someone violates those rules, they are considered abnormal at best and a threat at worst. These values make up our ethnic borders.

HELP ME UNDERSTAND

Our personal identities are loaded with preconceived notions based on our societal and unique selves. But if we are to lead in multi-ethnicity, we want our borders to be flexible. One of my mentors, the late Glen Kehrein, taught me to master asking the question: "Would you help me understand?" Border flexibility consists of learning how ethnicity shapes both us and our views of others.

People often mistake the one way forward as to become an ethnic search engine of some sort, gathering as many bits and pieces of information about different ethnicities as humanly possible. That is the way to prepare for an SAT test, not real life. Gathering information is important but is only part of the equation of understanding. True understanding comes from combining our heads (information) with our hearts (emotions) with our hands (experience). All three together lead the way forward.

A Journey of Understanding

In order to expand your borders, you need to take many personal journeys of understanding. I'm not talking about venturing out on some quest to find a person of color to befriend. And I am *especially* not talking about pressuring people ethnically different from you who you have hired to become your fishing buddy. I've had people ask me to be their friend specifically in order to learn more about my culture.

Who wants to be somebody's learning project? It doesn't work that way. I'm advocating making personal life adjustments—becoming an intentional learner for the sake of the kingdom.

When I planted River of Life, one of the first lay leaders, Pete, drove his family forty minutes one way to attend the church. One day I asked him why he did that. He told me about the journey of understanding his family was on. He and his wife Jamie from time to time took in boarders at their house. They lived in a somewhat rural place and had plenty of room to be hospitable. On one occasion, they had an African-American young lady look at a spare room. They felt good about her and decided to let her move in. Over dinner they discussed the situation with their kids. One of them did not sign off. When asked why, the kid said, "I don't know if I like black people." This threw Jamie and Pete for a loop. They decided they had to do something about the ethnic values of their kids. Their solution was to enroll their family to help me plant a multi-ethnic, inner-city church, where they faithfully served. It was much more than a "friendship project"; it was a lifestyle change.

When you isolate yourself within your own ethnic borders, you develop huge blind spots to the views of others. More than likely this means continual reinforcing of negative stereotypes. Trying to lead multi-ethnicity from that perspective is like the blind leading the blind.

If you want to go on a journey of understanding about married life, is it rational to exclusively hang with a tribe of single people?

I think not. You would want to hang with people who are successfully married, and as you encounter differences from your single status worldview, ask for understanding to gain insight into marriage. It's the same with ethnic learning.

Let me share a present journey of understanding I am on. I desire to flex my border and understand immigration from the perspective of my Latino colleagues. In doing so, I came across the story of Juan and Maria (not their real names). Their patchwork life in their native Mexico consisted of working long hours at whatever jobs they could find. When their first child was born, illegally crossing the border seemed the most logical move for a better life. After all, American companies were recruiting Mexicans to work. But a legal work visa took years to obtain, and the baby didn't have years to wait for food, clothing, and shelter. Juan and Maria chose to slip into California, find jobs, and start anew.

Soon, friends in their new land invited them to church, where Juan and Maria met Christ. Salvation changed their worldview and not having legal documentation bothered them. So they entered the process to become documented, legal workers. As the process continued, two more children came along, and a cousin's invitation prompted a move to the Midwest, where they found a new church family. But a routine traffic stop changed everything. When the police checked Juan's identification card, his name matched that of a wanted felon. By the time his innocence was clarified, the Immigration and Naturalization

Service had been called, and within a few days, Juan was deported back to Mexico. Maria was (and still is) struggling, to say the least.

The baby who inspired them to cross the border, now a teen, traded her dreams of college for the reality of working and helping to parent her siblings. Who is at fault? Juan and Maria for immigrating? The companies that lured them? The two churches involved in their lives? Government bureaucrats? In my journey, I've became aware of the need for economic and civil law to be reconciled . . . and soon.

I would never have arrived at that understanding by exclusively listening to the politicians and "talking heads" on TV that inform my societal self. I would also have never gotten there by discussing immigration exclusively with my black colleagues. The journey has been totally guided by my Latino friends. I have been given the gift of a unique perspective, and this has driven me to examine the whole issue scripturally, reforming my biblical self.

Authentic Community

The vehicle for journeys of understanding is authentic friendship and community. When I say this, people often have visions of all races holding hands and singing "Kum Ba Yah" around the campfire. But that's not what I mean. I mean having long-term, true, organic friendships where you can experience sincere community with others who are not ethnically the same as you. It's by far the most effective way to learn about and become more comfortable with differences.

Leaders have a tendency to think they understand someone who is ethnically different because they may regularly watch TV shows, read books, or listen to certain musical genres. That might be helpful, depending on the content you watch, read, or listen to. I encourage this type of learning, but it's basic learning. Advanced learning only comes through relationship. If you study Spanish for three years in high school, it doesn't translate into understanding what it means to be Mexican.

You will read in the next chapter how one of the historical effects of racialization is distrust. When you regularly interact with people ethnically different through authentic relationship, it changes your values, attitudes, and beliefs about life. This creates the glue to form bonds of trust. It brings about understanding to help you deal with the inevitable ethnic conflicts that will arise as you lead. If you have no skin in the game, when you hear about hurt and sorrow that has been caused by racialization, you have a tendency to not care as much. Because of the journey of Juan and Maria, I will never again view immigration as an impersonal issue.

Being a part of a sincere community of people who are ethnically different from you, as an organic part of your life, makes you fully conscious of the world you live in. It is a remarkable learning lab where you remove ethnic blind-spots. You learn how *not* to do and say painful and offensive things. You learn what intentional things you can do to be fruitful. You become a natural-born swimmer, like a fish in water, easily adjusting your thinking to be more inclusive.

Authentic Conversations

Besides long-term authentic relationships, the next best way to expand borders is through authentic conversations. This occurs naturally in long-term friendships and community, but at times there may be temporary God appointments made for you where you can gain insight. Pray and look for them. I denounce ethnic "friendship projects" but highly encourage constructive conversations that might lead to friendships. The more of these conversations you have, the more you learn about yourself and others.

To be open to potential God appointments, we need to stop placing troops at our ethnic borders. We can't assume everyone who is ethnically different from us is out to get us. Yes, racialization exists but it doesn't mean everyone has ulterior motives. Scripture does not teach that morality is based on ethnicity. We cannot have an us-versus-them mentality and expect any sort of success. Everyone cannot be a suspect.

I once participated with an evangelism training team, and a session was led by a slightly plump white man from Arkansas. His southern drawl was fierce. I'm ashamed to say it, but the term *redneck* immediately popped into my head when I met him. My ethnic troops were assembling at the border, and I only knew the guy for thirty seconds! I was sure he was a raving racist. As God would have it, the man sat right next to me at lunch break. I was looking for the escape hatch but was stuck. After introductions, he pulled out his wallet and showed me pictures of his grandkids, who looked African-American.

It turns out that his daughter was married to a black guy. As I talked to him, I found that he was a tremendously progressive thinker on race. I ended up learning a lot from him. After the interaction, I whispered a quiet prayer of repentance for being so narrow-minded.

Common Ground

Most differences based on ethnicity are not morally inappropriate. Each ethnicity elevates certain values above others. As an African-American Christian, let's say I drew a circle that represented my values. Then somebody who is a Christian of a different ethnicity drew one that represented his or hers. Chances are that our circles would significantly overlap. Chances are also that there would be some values that we do not have in common based on our ethnic backgrounds. The question then becomes: Do we have so little in common that we cannot build a relationship with one another? My guess would be that, most of the time, we have enough in common to build a relationship.

BORDER EXPANSION

Bridge builders recognize that differences exist, but they learn successful approaches for resolving conflict. They make border expansion part of their DNA by obtaining knowledge and applying it to their everyday living. They also provide spaces for significant communication to occur to keep misunderstandings based on ethnicity to a minimum.

Don't fall into the trap of thinking that treating everyone the same is somehow biblical. This may sound good, but it is not good practice. At times we must consider ethnicity in order to have successful relationships.

I knew of Christian leaders who claimed to want to reach a first-generation Latino community yet planned to cancel the Spanish broadcasts on the church's radio station. The broadcasts were considered special treatment of Latinos. I don't know how you reach an entire people group but don't plan to speak their primary language! These leaders changed their plans once their Latino constituents found out and expressed their displeasure. What these leaders initially forgot to do was to embrace the principle that ethnicity shapes our lives, and they forgot to make the adaptations necessary to further the kingdom. This is the most practical step that a ministry needs to take in order to practice reconciliation.

Adaptation based on certain needs is not a foreign concept. Youth pastors regularly adapt in order to spread the gospel in a way youth understand. Fund-raising consultants are often hired to help communicate clearly to people with financial resources to give generously. For some reason, when it comes to ethnic concerns, some see making special accommodations as wrong.

We must change that way of thinking.

NOTES

1. Cardinal Joseph Bernadin, *The Gift of Peace* (New York: Doubleday, 1997), 14.

2. Andrew Walls, *The Missionary Movement in Christian History: Studies in the Transmission of Faith* (Maryknoll, N.Y.: Orbis, 1996), 53.

RACIALIZATION

Every successful multi-ethnic Christian organization I know of has one key operating principle that my dad inadvertently taught me in 1977 when I was seven years old. I call it an "obvious secret," which of course is a contradiction. How can a secret be obvious? I use this paradoxical description because people genuinely don't seem to know (like a secret), but it hides in broad daylight.

I was in second grade and had a book report due on cheetahs. I read a book on them and wrote until my little fingers were sore, scratching out one fine page. My dad read it over and asked me what the assignment requirement was. I said, "Read a book on an animal and write a one-page report."

He replied, "Then you're not done. Write another page."

I wondered aloud why I had to do an extra page. After all, I completed the assignment requirement. Wasn't that enough? His response is still seared in my brain, and quite frankly, it has been a guiding principle for me throughout my life: "Son, you might as well get used to it. You will always have to do extra as a black man to make it in this world. Always remember you're black."

RACE EQUALS ETHNICITY

Eventually, I'll let you in on the secret. But before I do, let me address an issue that many of you who are veterans of this discussion may have already picked up on about this book. You may have noticed I use *race* and *ethnicity* interchangeably. When I do so with my presentations, it never fails that someone rises up and challenges me on doing this.

Theoretically, race is the result of categorizing people genetically, and ethnicity is the result of categorizing people by shared history, cultural roots, and a sense of shared identity. But this book is about practicality, and most of the people you lead probably do not differentiate between race and ethnicity. These two terms mean the same thing to most people, so we will operate with that perspective. It may be helpful to see how these terms have become intertwined.

The "race as genetics" scientific narrative has proven to be an inept way to sort people. (I'll talk more about this in the next section.) Academics searched for new ways of classifying people, and the one that prevailed was ethnicity. Popularized beginning in the 1920s and 1930s, *ethnicity* is generally defined as a type of cultural identity in which a person identifies with a particular people group. Ethnic groups are people who share a common sense of "peoplehood" (language, nationality, etc.). Here is the tricky part—racial genetic characteristics (from the old way of thinking) are also considered a part of an ethnic identity.

Ethnicity sorts people based on differences in social characteristics rather than genetic characteristics. Race has moved into that realm as well, as most social scientists now call race a social construct. So instead of emphasizing genetic differences, the emphasis now lies in studying differences in culture (religion, language, nationality, politics, customs, etc.). But genetic differences like skin color and eye shape still remain a part of the ethnic narrative, although not as important as they had previously been perceived.

The result of the shift is that definitions of *race* and *ethnicity* have become moving targets. They are ever changing. For instance, did you know that at one time the Irish were considered a separate race? Or Latinos were once considered white? Or one can be considered black in America but white in Brazil? It's because there is no one-size-fits-all universal definition.

Therefore, as Christians we must proceed with caution as we utilize the language given to us by society. Both terms—*race* and *ethnicity*—still incorporate failed racial science to some extent. Even within the ethnic narrative, the world is divided into white and nonwhite, with *white* replacing *Caucasian* as the gold standard. Within this narrative, there is still potential for everybody not to have equal seating at the table of humanity. The ethnic part of our identities is not only individually defined, but also projected onto us by society.

Once I was talking with a very influential Christian leader. During our conversations, he told me—point blank—that race isn't that big of a deal. "The culture has moved on," he said.

I could not disagree more.

My second-generation Korean friend, David, grew up in the US. English is his native language, but he will unapologetically say to you that he does not consider himself anything less than an Asian-American. This is because he has been spat on, beaten, kicked, and ridiculed for being Korean. But he is not ashamed to be part of an ethnic group that God loves and intends to bring into the kingdom. To tell someone like David that "the culture has moved on" is to deny his life experience.

We must accept that race is an influencer of American life. In fact, there may not be another country in the world where race plays such a central role. Racial discrimination became a way of life within our foundational institutions (governmental, economic, religious, familial, and educational). America's historical record suggests that we should start with the premise that race influences everything we do in society, including leading Christian organizations. It is just a matter of how we manage that influence.

SKIN DEEP

It is critical that we grasp the concept that skin color is only skin deep. The genetic makeup that determines your skin color has absolutely nothing to do with predicting musical or athletic talent, intellectual ability, or any other behavioral trait. Really, it's kind of crazy that this kind of thinking is the conventional wisdom.[1]

Recently, I was talking to a very godly and smart friend of mine. We were discussing a mutual acquaintance we had in common who happened to be a Chinese-American. Out of the blue, my friend said, "They [meaning Chinese] have different brains than us. They are really, really smart." And she wasn't joking.

I emphatically stressed that, although she might not know any less-intelligent Chinese people personally, if she took a trip to Beijing, that way of thinking wouldn't hold up. Intellect is not rooted in skin color. My friend meant no harm in her comments, but we cannot continue to think this way. Racial thinking goes something like this:

Person A is from (fill in the blank) ethnic group; person B is from (same ethnic group); therefore persons A and B automatically inherit a host of attributes and are the same across the board. This kind of thinking can be dangerous.

And really, it makes no rational sense. What if I told you all blue cars were the same? It doesn't matter whether it is a BMW, Chevy, Toyota, or Kia—if they are blue, they are the same. I would guess you would think I wasn't very knowledgeable about cars. Yes, the color of the car tells us something about it, but it only tells us is what color it is. The color of the car is just one aspect of the identity of the car. It would serve us well to apply the same standard to people.

I can't tell you the number of times people have expressed mild shock because I thought and acted differently concerning certain life views than other African-Americans they know. Or to be honest, the mild shock I experience at times when I find out a white or non-black person takes a contrarian position to the "typical" thought of some-one in their same racial group. Why the shock?

The answer requires a brief history lesson on the idea of race. We've all been conditioned in a certain way of thinking that is not based in truth. The concept of categorizing and sorting is natural to our exis-tence as human beings. Recall that one of the first activities Adam was required to do by God was to classify (Gen. 2:19–20). Together Adam and Eve defined the relationships (father, mother, son, etc.) that had origins in their union as the first human couple to occupy the earth.

For centuries, people have been categorized by geographic region of origin, religious beliefs, wealth, social standing, language, and the like. Now, we just accept it as fact. Pick up any introductory social science textbook and you will find a definition of *race* running along the lines of a system that categorizes people based on physical characteristics. But you should know that this way of thinking has a relatively modern historical beginning and was not always (and still is not) universal to all societies. It wasn't until the Enlightenment that categorizing people into genetic groups was considered.

The world was introduced to the idea of race as a valid way to categorize people through the study of natural history and anthropology. Johann Blumenbach (1752–1840) is considered the grandfather of anthropology and is credited for popularizing a hierarchy scheme of humans that became the most prevalently used system. The heyday of such belief (at least scientifically) was the nineteenth century. Blumenbach and others were convinced they were advancing scientific knowledge by sorting people according to physical characteristics. Regardless of motives, their findings were typically used to build a hierarchy of human worth. The standard of racial science was from those who descended from European genetics, classified as Caucasians. All other races were to be compared to and exist in relation to their Caucasian-classified counterparts. The less you resembled the white biological standard and adapted this way of life, the less valuable you were under the racial system.

Common perception is that physical characteristics (skin color, eye color, body type, etc.) make us vastly different from one another. Ironically, *scientifically* it has been proven over and over again that there is no significant genetic difference between people who are classified in different biological racial categories. For example, if I need a blood transfusion, what matters most are my blood type and other genetic factors, not my skin color. Biologically speaking, there is just the human race, not different species of human beings. Modern-day social scientists pretty much dismiss the idea of race as biology as a sound scientific principle. In spite of this fact, the concept of race is still alive and well. Why? Simply put, because we think it exists.

Think of race as Santa Claus. For me Santa was real, and it didn't matter what anybody said most of my elementary school days. In fourth grade, my teacher had the class debate whether Santa exists. It was all the kids who believed in him versus all the nonbelievers. Despite all the "scientific" facts presented by the other side, all I knew was I sent a letter to the North Pole every December 1, and on December 25, all the toys I wanted were sitting in my living room under the Christmas tree.

I felt so sorry for those poor, misguided, Santa-haters. (Of course, we all know who was misguided.) By sixth grade, I knew that the only place Santa existed was in people's minds, which is the same address of race. Nevertheless, race isn't as harmless as Santa. In spite of the fact that race is only skin deep, has been genetically disproven, and only exists in our minds, it has very real implications.

DEFINING THE CHALLENGE

There exists a horrible history of those ethnic groups with political power generally oppressing ethnic minorities. Throughout America's history, race has been used to justify enslaving Africans, conquering Native Americans, rejecting Asian immigrants, and seizing Mexican lands. Sadly, that's the tip of the United States' racial historical iceberg. One can't do an honest reading of American history and not see how racial classification has been used to oppress entire groups of people.

In modern society, race affects housing, neighborhoods, socioeconomic status, health, criminal justice, mortality rates, religion—the list is endless. Sociologists call this phenomena or "racialization." As stated in the introduction, a racialized society is a society wherein race profoundly matters for differences in life experiences, life opportunities, and social relationships. It is one that allocates different economic, political, social, and psychological rewards to groups along racial lines. Basically, it is the process in which people impose a racial element into a social situation, often to oppress people.

I'm asking that we impose it for self-awareness. Let me be blunt and tell you where the problem lies. Despite the avalanche of historical evidence about the role race has and continues to play in causing disparities in our society, many want to believe we live in a colorblind world. Because of racialization, color blindness is not an option.

Connecting Belief and Behavior

As Christians we are a cultural montage made up of many different ethnicities, social classes, and political views. The glue that holds us all together is that we believe the Bible is the final authority on how we should live. We are people of truth and righteousness. But race has proven to be an extremely hard thing to transcend.

I have taught many racial diversity workshops steeped in theological principles. I would say 95 percent of participants would agree that it is the biblical course of action to work toward multi-ethnicity. So if everybody pretty much agrees theologically, integrating our organizations is no sweat, right? Well, if it were that easy you probably wouldn't be reading this book!

Right belief does not automatically equal right action. If the Bible is so explicit about embracing ethnic diversity and if one of the major tenets of Christianity is living out the principles of the Bible, then why is there such a consistent theological disconnect among Christians to follow this biblical ethic?

The obvious secret is that race matters and must be taken into account. Dad's primary lesson to me when I wrote my book report was not on racial prejudice, a favorable or unfavorable view of a person based on stereotypes, or racism, a system of advantage or disadvantage based on race. It was based on a subtle but much deeper observation on American life. School was in session on the *meaning* of race and how I was to respond to it.

Overcoming Historical Distrust

My dad gave me the advice he did because of his distrust of societal institutions based on his experience with them. He felt the full weight of racialization growing up in Anniston, Alabama, during the height of Jim Crow America. One of the many repercussions was that he dropped out of high school—in part because the segregated school system tried to force him to be a house painter or factory worker and he wasn't mechanically inclined. He was more academically oriented, and it was made perfectly clear to him that little black boys should not dream of growing up and going to college. I am happy to say that Dad overcame this and ended up going to night school for ten years, earning a GED and two bachelor's degrees. But his overcoming obstacles to achieve success should not excuse what was done to him from a societal perspective.

Managing Moral Choices

As leaders we must morally manage and define what ethnicity means within our personal lives and the organizations we lead. It is impossible to overestimate the importance of this basic realization about leading toward multi-ethnicity.

What is meant by moral management? Morality is one of the major things that makes us human. Animals typically don't make moral decisions; they react to the environment around them. We are different because, at the core, we are moral beings with other dimensions that reflect this core. It's why the apostle Paul said that following Christ is the best way to live, because he will teach us the most holy way (1 Cor. 11:1). Living Christ's way provides the answers to questions like: Who am I? Why am I here? What really matters in life?

We know as Christian leaders that the material world is not all there is to reality. So we find platforms to express our inner moral yearnings. Moral expression happens physically, cognitively, emotionally, spiritually, and socially. These are morality's pragmatic aspects. Therefore, we start food pantries and thrift shops for the poor, divorce support groups for our communities, and even build institutions of higher learning as tangible demonstrations of our moral urges.

Because we live in a racialized society, dismissing ethnic identity through color blindness is akin to taking an immoral action. I realize this is a strong statement, so let me briefly give you my reasoning behind it. First, God created us with different skin tones. It was not an accident; it was his intent. To say that you don't see my skin color means you are ignoring what God created. Second, the atrocities that have been committed throughout history based on race speak for themselves. Humans have taken what God meant for good (diverse skin color) and perverted it for evil. For centuries skin color has been a cause for a tremendous amount of human conflict. Some have no idea how their racial background naturally forms a basis for distrust. And it is almost unavoidable to at least partly misjudge the actions of people based on falsely learned racial expectations. All this has to be managed rather than ignored by practicing color blindness.

Reducing Confusion and Polarization

When racialization is concealed by practicing color blindness, it results in confusion at best, and, more often, polarization. People can't get on the same page. Instead of productive dialogue, we get schizophrenic, emotionally charged conversations based on racism, prejudice, and historical distrust, which fail to reflect the good intentions of our hearts. This leads to fatigue. People just flat-out get tired of engaging.

I've coached many skilled leaders who begin with the mythological premise that all white people (particularly males) are evil, rich, and guilty, and all ethnic people are moral, poor, or dying to have a white friend. And in many ministries, if you aren't black or white, there is no room for your ideas and concerns. My Latino, Asian, and Native American friends have often told me stories of being excluded from the reconciliation mix altogether. The point is that race matters (whether we acknowledge it or not), so why not intentionally explore what it means for us both personally and organizationally?

Confronting Unrealistic Idealism

If I had a dollar for every time somebody said to me, "Alvin, I don't see a black man; I just see a man," I would be very wealthy!

I understand that most Christians really want to live in a color-blind world, but we can't let desires and good intentions overrule the reality of the meaning of race in America. The reality is that color blindness is too idealistic. The primary assumption underlying such a stance is extremely flawed.

Color blindness assumes it is possible for us to operate out of a space that is not ethnically influenced. People have pushed back at me when presenting my views on color blindness by saying I am not accounting for the work of the Holy Spirit. My response is yes, Jesus transforms our hearts and views on race . . . if we let him. But we won't let him if we're convinced it's not a problem.

We do have free will and can operate on our own autonomy, which is why even though we are saved and on our way to heaven, we are still capable of sin. In fact, I consider determining the meaning of race in our lives a part of our sanctification process.

Reconsidering the meaning of race is part of the renewing of our minds. (See Acts 6:1–7, 10–15 for biblical case studies on mind renewal concerning ethnic divisions.) The president of my denomination and my boss, William Hamel, often tells the story of his grandfather being part of the KKK. Some serious spiritual renewal had to happen across generational lines in order for him to have a healthy, biblical view of the role of race.

Acting with Intentionality

We cannot afford to be blind to race as ambassadors of reconciliation. Therefore, to successfully lead people to manage the meaning of race, it must be intentional. We must then lead people in reconsidering its meaning within the context of grace, hope, and love.

Have you looked at demographics lately? Ethnic groups are outgrowing the white population mainly because of immigration and birthrates. The trend may be new to you, but it is not new to demographers. They have been observing this development for years. In the not-too-distant future, we will have to rethink what the terms *majority* and *minority* mean, because they are rapidly being redefined. The new term is *majority-minority*, meaning the majority of people will be ethnic minorities. Consider the following statistics:

- The Latino population, already the nation's largest minority group, will triple in size and account for most of the nation's population growth from 2005 through 2050. Hispanics will make up 29 percent of the US population in 2050, compared with 14 percent in 2005.[2]
- The non-Hispanic white population will increase more slowly than other racial and ethnic groups; whites will become a minority (47 percent) by 2050.[3]
- Since 2000, the percentage of the total US population that is nonwhite has changed from 31 percent to 37 percent. The

change is accelerating among the younger ages. In fifteen years, among those under age forty-five, the percentage of nonwhites will exceed that of whites. For those under eighteen, that change will happen in six years.[4]

All this adds up to a picture where ethnic groups are younger than whites, so they are more likely to be having and raising children. They will continue to be the population growth driver of our country.

For years I have told Christian organizations they need to prepare because diversity is coming. That is no longer accurate; diversity is here. As our country becomes increasingly more racially diverse, how can we be more inclusive? If Christian leaders aren't putting this question at the forefront of their strategic planning, they are flat out being negligent.

Rice University sociologist Michael O. Emerson cites recent research that states 92.5 percent of churches in the United States are racially segregated. In fact, his studies indicate that churches today are ten times more segregated than the neighborhoods in which they sit and twenty times more segregated than nearby public schools.[5] How can we truly say we are being missional if we aren't addressing our nation's demographic shift?

During my years of working with many different Christian organizations, I have observed a developing trend. These organizations are losing some of their effectiveness because of an inability to embrace the rapidly changing demographics. Because of demographics, developing demographically relevant leaders must become an expected norm in Christian institutions of all types. These are leaders who effectively interact in an ethnically diverse society. There must be a basic understanding of racialization and how it affects us.

I am convinced from years of teaching, preaching, and consulting within Christian contexts that if we are going to continue to be effective we must be able to balance solid theological belief with effective social analysis. My experience has been that the main reasons people don't embrace a multi-ethnic paradigm lies not in their theology but in their inability to follow the example of the "men of Issachar, who understood the times and knew what Israel should do" (1 Chron. 12:32).

FIVE PRINCIPLES OF SEEING COLOR

The most common question I receive after imploring people to see color is: "How can I see color and not stereotype?" Stereotypes are an inflated conviction that one would associate to certain groups of people. These beliefs are usually unfavorable and serve to keep certain people "out" and keep others "in." Whenever we say, "All _____ are _____," we are standing on unbiblical ground. When I talk about seeing color, I am talking about heightened self-awareness. Here are five principles to follow to keep from stereotyping.

Humility

Unchecked, racially arrogant attitudes are the quickest way to destructive stereotyping. People tend to frame humility as denigrating self, but that is not what I mean by humility. *Humility* means declining the temptation to put yourself in God's place. It means following Job's example and figuring out what it means to submit to God in his world. It means resting in the assurance that our number one identity is not in our races but in the grace of being children of God. Resting in this fact, there is no need to look down on others. There is also no need to have to prove yourself because of your race. Be comfortable in your own skin because God made you the ethnicity you are and that's enough. If people can't accept that, there is no need to declare war or become highly defensive in order to make yourself look good. Humility causes one to repent of ethnic arrogance and to reject seeking revenge for perceived slights.

Truth-Telling

Just before an important event, my wife, Caroline, grabbed me backstage and whispered, "Your fly is open." With her help, I discreetly prevented an embarrassing situation. What if she hadn't told me the truth? I would have been on stage and the crowd would not have heard a word I said. They would have been either too busy laughing or too uncomfortable to even look at me. She cared enough about me to tell me the truth. With people we truly care about, we're honest about what matters, regardless of how potentially offensive or embarrassing the situation may seem.

Every week Christians practice the art of "slightly" lying to each other. I call this the ritual of politeness. As a straight shooter, let me ask some basic questions to see if you have participated in this ritual. How many times have you told a preacher, "That sermon was fantastic" when it wasn't? Or complimented the worship leader and then on the drive home told your spouse how off-key his or her singing was? Or told someone, "Great dress" or "Sharp tie" when really you were thinking, "Wow, I'd never wear that"? We're all guilty. Of course, telling little white lies on trivial things such as these is not earth-shattering. In fact, I already know the standard defense: It's the "Christian" thing to do, because you don't want to hurt the other person's feelings. But I contend that for most people politeness is not the reason they skirt engaging the truth about race. The real reason is they want to protect themselves from conflict.

This natural reluctance must be overcome if you and your organization are going to make serious strides. The fear of being uncomfortable is what most hinders reconciliation efforts. If we refuse to speak the truth because of fear, we are operating as hypocrites. We may be polite hypocrites, but still hypocrites.

I'm not talking about using politically correct semantics — it goes deeper than that. Remember, language shapes how we view reality, and it reveals values. When someone tells me they don't see my skin color, that person's language reveals a disconnect with biblical truth. Didn't God create the different ethnicities in a way that we should notice? Then let's assume God knew what he was doing and not be afraid to acknowledge it.

Patience

Besides feeling uncomfortable, another big reason people avoid discussing race is because it can quickly become emotional. But it is OK to be emotional, as long as we keep our emotions in check so they don't become destructive or lead us to act in ways we shouldn't. This is much easier said than done.

I have often been the chief violator of this principle, but God has graciously helped me get better as the years pass. Early in my journey, I routinely blew up at people over racial issues. To be totally honest, every now and then I still do. I now realize that when it comes to racial issues, it takes time to "get it," and no one "gets it" overnight. We all need steadiness in this area. If we keep this in mind, it will go a long way in helping others realize the significance of racialization.

One thing that has helped me is the realization that people can make honest racial mistakes. They really don't know that what they said or did was hurtful. It is possible for someone to do or say something race-influenced but not be a racist. I work hard on giving people the benefit of the doubt. Matthew 18:15–17 is helpful to follow to achieve the patience needed.

Encouragement

Too much time is spent on the negative side of racial dynamics. There is a term called *jaundiced eye*, meaning to approach people with caution. I am contrarian on this. We have to work hard to suspend our root assumptions about people. If we don't, it will lead to stereotyping, which is not good. We need to be careful not to build an atmosphere filled with a constant diatribe on what is wrong while short-changing spending time on what is right or how to move forward. I won't end a conversation about bad racial dynamics until the other party and I have some dialogue about proposed solutions.

Sadly, I have come to believe that some people really don't want things to get better. There is power and comfort in always being the victim, the one who is always guilty. We have to learn to encourage one another in the Lord instead of always assigning blame or imagining slights. At some point, the focus has to be on getting better.

Respect

All ethnic groups need to be treated with dignity. One killer of reconciliation efforts is paternalism, the intrusion of one group on another against its will. The intrusion is justified by claiming that the group intruded upon will be "better off," resulting in a one-sided relationship.

As a former urban pastor, here is what paternalism looked like for me. At Christmastime I used to field phone calls from suburban pastors who wanted to donate clothes and toys to my former ministry. As much as I appreciated their goodwill, my standard answer was, "No, thanks. What I really need are women willing to build relationships with some of our single moms. I need tutors for kids. I need people who can have our folks over for dinner and vice versa in order to break down barriers." After many conversations along those lines, I am sad to report that only two churches ever took me up on my counteroffer. Unlike the church leadership in Jerusalem represented in Acts 6:1–7, most churches were not interested in a partnership that benefited all involved. Those suburban church leaders were only interested in meeting their needs at the expense of devaluing my church's needs. The two churches that took me up on my counteroffer still have a relationship with River of Life today, even though I've been gone for five years. Those pastors often said to me that their congregations received much more from the partnership than they ever anticipated. All were blessed, which is the way things should be.

THE GIFT OF TRUTH

Let me end this chapter with a story that models what seeing color looks like. After a presentation on cultural trends, I tapped the speaker on the shoulder as he sat down in his seat. During his talk, he mentioned how he was hindered by his "whiteness." He grew up in a middle-class, white suburb and knew very little of the world outside that lens. I offered to spend time with him during a break.

"Are you aware that all the faces on your slides were white?" was a simple question I asked. How ironic on a presentation on cultural trends, where the biggest trend of all is our changing demographics! The reality was that both his slides and presentation exclusively demonstrated a white person's view of the world. He was quiet for a moment.

We went on to discuss his comments during the presentation about hip-hop. The musical genre had captured his attention so much that he seriously thought about pursuing it as his next academic research interest. He suspected that hip-hop had the same (if not more) impact on culture as postmodernism.

Patiently, I walked him through the ways in which hip-hop, starting as an African-American cultural expression, developed into a global force. I could tell he was enjoying the talk immensely as he took notes at a frantic pace. At one point, he stopped and sighed, "I can't believe how blind I was to all this." He then said something very profound: "Thank you for the gift of truth."

This encounter is one I hope takes place a hundred times over. It is a prime example of how we can see color and leverage difference. We need to take the knowledge of our life experience and enlighten those who are blind to it. It offers a powerful cure to color blindness that tends to go together with our Christian faith, removing the barriers of leading toward God's multi-ethnic kingdom.

NOTES

1. I recommend two resources to learn more about race and racialization. The first is a three-part video documentary series: *Race: The Power of an Illusion* (California Newsreel, 2003), from http://news reel.org/video/RACE-THE-POWER-OF-AN-ILLUSION. The second is Charles A. Gallagher, *Rethinking the Color Line: Readings in Race and Ethnicity* (New York: McGraw-Hill, 2009).

2. Pew Research Social and Demographic Trends, Executive Summary, accessed February 25, 2013, http://www.pewsocial trends.org/2008/02/11/us-population-projections-2005-2050/.

3. Ibid.

4. "Changing Faces," *USA Today*, January 18–20, 2013, weekend edition.

5. Cited in Mark DeYmaz, "Growing Churches Just Like Us," *Outreach Magazine*, July/August 2011, 97.

UNINTENTIONALITY

Regardless of how godly the founders of your organization were, if they didn't account for multi-ethnicity in the original vision, they didn't think multi-ethnicity was relevant. I realize that is a strong statement, but it serves to make a point. Until decision-makers intentionally begin to implement multi-ethnic correctives, most people will continue to see it as unimportant to the organization.

When an organization lacks intentionality about multi-ethnicity, it will create an idealistically distorted atmosphere. People will wear rose-colored glasses. Many assume that once we are saved all ethnic issues are magically solved. And when decision-makers are unintentional about multi-ethnicity, a false sense of security will set in. People will assume there are no problems with ethnic diversity within your organization and no need to address it.

Most people seem to think that if there is a race problem it's because people are prejudiced, which of course they feel they are not. Most would agree there were problems in the past with race in the US, but not now. Oftentimes scapegoats ("race baiters," media, government, liberals, etc.) are mentioned to justify their position. The problem lies everywhere but with them or their organization.

Extra grace is required when leading change in this area. It's hard for people to bring themselves to believe the realities of racialization, and some never will in spite of your best efforts. In their minds, there is not a reality to racism but just *perceived* realities. Racialization is like a bad cold, something people just have to get over. Our response to this type of attitude is critical.

When you start being intentional about multi-ethnicity, keep in the back of your mind that it's like premarital counseling. Most couples have blinders on concerning marriage. When I was pastoring, my job was to take off those blinders so the couple could face the reality of the challenge marriage brings. It's our role as leaders to do the same by being intentional.

THE ROLE OF FOUNDING DNA

Founding DNA is the distinguishing doctrine of your particular Christian tradition mixed with the intent of the founder(s) of your particular organization. This DNA is what makes your organization unique within the broader Christian world. This combination plays a huge role in either helping or hindering when it comes to your integration efforts.

I recently heard a presentation where the speaker mentioned that globally we have anywhere from thirty thousand to fifty thousand different denominations. The number is staggering. Each one of those groups reflects the spirit of whoever founded them. For example, even though John Calvin and Martin Luther passed away long ago, their ideas live on through institutions that consider themselves a part of their respective traditions. Think of it as the "consciousness" of your organization. If you work at an organization rooted in the charismatic tradition, there are things that would only be understood if you are familiar with being a charismatic. The same could be said for Southern Baptists, Presbyterians, Jesuits, etc. Typically, the apple doesn't fall too far from the founding tree.

It's your founding DNA that forms the base of your organizational identity. Remember from the ethnic borders chapter that by *identity* I mean the way we present who we are to others as well as ourselves. Previously, I focused more on how this affects us personally. In this chapter, we will focus on the organizational level.

If you are a decision-maker at a church, Christian college, or non-profit, you probably share something in common with many other Christian organizations in regards to multi-ethnicity. Your founders probably did not intentionally account for ethnocentrism. The typical trend is that, whatever the racial practices of the day were, our organizations mirrored them.

I once used Martin Luther King, Jr. as a positive example in a discussion. One person said I shouldn't do that because King's theology was too liberal. I looked up the policies of this person's place of employment at the time King was in seminary, and it revealed that they practiced racial segregation during that time period. I let the person know that maybe King was theologically liberal because many conservative theological schools (like his) weren't interested in educating him. We agreed it was a missed institutional opportunity to leverage diversity.

How can a school claim to represent Christianity while at the same time implementing policies that discriminate on the basis of race? For the longest time, being a promoter for multi-ethnicity was considered to be siding with the liberal "social gospel." For many years, evangelicals seemed to oppose multi-ethnicity, not for biblical reasons, but mainly because liberal Christians were in favor of it. Historically speaking, it is a relatively recent development that being for multi-ethnicity has been generally perceived as a good thing for theological conservatives.

To demonstrate how founding DNA can affect an organization, I will present two examples from my past. First, on September 23, 1924, the Cincinnati Bible Seminary (now Cincinnati Christian University) came into existence through the merging of two institutions that had begun one year earlier. McGarvey Bible College in Louisville, Kentucky, and Cincinnati Bible Institute in Cincinnati, Ohio, were similar in purpose and belief.

Cincinnati Bible Seminary came into being to meet the pressing leadership needs of the Restoration Movement at that time. The founding principle and ultimate purpose of the school was to train church leaders who were well-grounded in the Word of God. This was especially important, since infidelity toward the Scripture was corrupting many church-sponsored institutions of higher education at the time.

The founders wrote a bylaw stating that the president, the vice president, and all full-time faculty members are required to be members of an independent Christian church or Church of Christ. This seems reasonable and harmless on the surface—until you view it through the lens of multi-ethnicity.

While I worked for them, the board asked me what their biggest hindrance was to integrating the full-time faculty, and I pointed out the previously mentioned bylaw. Trying to find a full-time professor of color under those conditions was like asking the dean to find someone who has a doctorate in guitar to teach math. It can be done, but what a barrier!

Consider that only a small percentage of the population has a doctorate. That group grows smaller based on whatever specialization the school is looking for. Then the group gets slimmed even more if you want someone who is nonwhite. The pool of candidates shrinks further when you factor in that they have to be Christian. And not just any Christian, but one who specifically comes from a Restoration Movement (independent Church of Christ) background. Now, if you want to be multi-ethnic, you are talking about fishing in a puddle. And we haven't even gotten into other important factors like whether they want to live in Cincinnati, salary, or fit within the campus culture. With all of this in mind, it is no small feat to integrate full-time faculty as long as that bylaw stands.

I give the founders of the school the benefit of the doubt. I don't believe for one second they were intentionally trying to be ethnocentric when they drafted the bylaw. From what I could discern, the intent was to protect the school from "going liberal" so to speak (which, if you know your American church history, was a huge concern during the time period the school was founded [1924]). They also have what is called a non-creedal tradition, demonstrated by the slogan: "No creed but Christ, no book but the Bible." In other words, the founders were not too keen on statements of faith to sign. So they enacted what they believed was in the best interests of their school, which was to require Church of Christ membership. Their good intention was to keep the school theologically conservative. But as I demonstrated, they unintentionally created a massive barrier for the school to reach its goal of an ethnically integrated full-time faculty.

A second example comes from my first full-time ministry experience at a Christian nonprofit organization called City Cure. This was a nonprofit ministry serving at-risk youth through one-on-one, relationship-based programs. The founders were a group of people who believed in life-on-life ministry and personal support-raising for salary purposes. They also believed in communal living in the heart of the inner-city neighborhood they served.

They worked extremely hard to find nonwhite staff, doing a nationwide search for a director. But no one would sign on. It wasn't because of City Cure's vision or mission but because of the founding DNA of personal support-raising. Unintentionally, the founders put nonwhites at a disadvantage. Many ethnic groups are not familiar with the concept of personal support-raising and did not have the personal relationships required to hit financial goals. This is a common integration challenge in organizations that follow this philosophy.

Both of these examples were of organizations with founders who had good intentions in doing ministry but never considered that they might be setting up ethnocentric systems of operation. They had unknowingly created barriers of exclusion. Of course, there are some Christian organizations that are not quite so innocent. In either case, the results are similar—ethnic exclusion.

WHAT TIME IS IT?

Leading with racial transcendence seems to always start with a *kairos* moment. Time is described a few ways in the Bible. There is *chronos*, which is time marching on. It is measured in seconds, minutes, hours, days, months, and years. Then there is *kairos*. It refers to the right time for something to happen, a season in life. That is your birthday, your wedding date, or Christmas. It is a time set apart for carrying out a special task.

Perhaps the demographics of the neighborhood around the ministry have changed, and your church wants to become multi-ethnic in order to serve the community better. Maybe your child has married someone of a different race, or you just returned from a mission trip and your eyes have been opened to a whole new world. It could be that nasty racial incidents at your campus or nonprofit have caused you to pause and think about the state of race relations in the twenty-first century. In my experience, while Christian leaders are usually familiar with the term *racial reconciliation*, most have not thought deeply about how it fits within their faith walk or leadership philosophy. The time is right to do so.

Evolution of Ethnic Consciousness[1]

Time Period	Ethnic Era	Societal Era	Conventional Wisdom
Before 1950	Segregation	Legal Separation	Nonwhite is "less than."
1950s	Desegregation	Legal Corrective	Nonwhite is disadvantaged.
1960s	Integration	Legal Corrective	Nonwhite is missing.
1970s	Multiculturalism	Social Justice	More identities than race vie for status.
1980s	Cultural Diversity	Economic	Racial identity is "watered down."
1990s	Cultural Competence	Humanism	Race is one of many identity categories.
2000s	Globalization	Necessity	Race is an afterthought.

Prior to 1950, the norm was segregation. Once our groundbreaking civil rights legislation took effect, the journey to integration and equal rights began in earnest. The force behind change during both the 1950s and 1960s was mainly legal in nature. With legal victories, a new paradigm began to take shape in the 1970s called multiculturalism. From a societal standpoint, this was a significant worldview transition. Prior to the 1970s, the spotlight had been on assimilation into an American melting pot, a metaphor for all melting into mainstream culture. Mainstream culture usually meant white, Protestant, male, heterosexual, and upper middle class.

With the emergence of multiculturalism, people questioned the appropriateness of asking everyone to assimilate to one standard. A new metaphor began to emerge: a salad. As with the ingredients in a salad, each culture keeps its distinctive characteristics and adds its unique flavor to the meal. Tomatoes remain tomatoes; lettuce remains lettuce; and croutons remain croutons. The tomato never asks the crouton to act more like a tomato. The tomato demands that the croutons and lettuce make room for it in the salad bowl.

People of color began to assert their unique flavor within the American landscape. In addition, other primary identities, such as women, religions outside of Christianity, homosexual-identified, and others, began to assert their right to a seat at the societal table. The new metaphor of a salad began to prevail, and by the 1980s, cultural diversity began to be the new normal.

Corporate America discovered it was good business to market based on ethnicity, gender, and other distinct cultural categories that were emerging. Many companies and school systems implemented cultural-diversity training in earnest for their employees. For a corporation, it just made good business sense. For a school system that might have fifty different ethnicities, a plurality of religions represented, and a percentage of parents who were homosexual-identified among its student population, it was a move of survival.

By the 1990s, cultural competence was a must. Cultural competency is the art and science of intentional interaction with other cultural groups. From a Christian perspective, it is not a coincidence that predominantly white Christian groups, such as Promise Keepers, began to focus on the topic of racial reconciliation. They and many others sensed the signs of the times.

Like the shift to multiculturalism in the 1970s, we are now in the midst of a paradigm shift into globalization. *Globalization* is a catchall term that describes how foundational social institutions of the world (political, economic, familial, religious, and educational) are moving toward forming global citizens. The challenge at hand is to function together in unity in spite of our differences. Multicultur-alism was all about establishing identity, whereas globalization is about existing with mixed identities. As organizational leaders, we must pay attention to this shift.

In Wichita, Kansas, I addressed this topic with hundreds of church leaders, mainly from Nebraska, Kansas, and Missouri. When I would ask a leader where he or she was from, the opening comment always seemed to be, "It's in the middle of nowhere, but I'm from . . ." Why would church leaders from the middle of nowhere—tiny towns not known for ethnic diversity—want to hear about multi-ethnic challenges?

A common narrative was how their towns were being flooded by people from all over the world, mainly due to the decisions of global corporations. The typical story was that the town was all white and losing people, and then a factory of some sort was built nearby, and within five to ten years, the town was integrated with people of color from some other country. The "other" people were quickly becoming the majority.

I illustrated in chapter 2 what our present and future demographics are. For the first time in history, ethnic birthrates surpass white ones. The smart decision-maker knows that if you want to be effective in the present, you need to operate like it's the future. I know a pastor in Florence, Kentucky, who translates his worship service from English to Japanese. Why? Toyota has its North American manufacturing headquarters nearby, and they are taking advantage of the opportunity to bring the gospel to the executive management who work there. That's a prime example of how globalization should affect our organizational practice. God is in the middle of bringing the world to our doorstep. Is your organization ready?

My friend Allen grew up in the Midwest. While globalization had changed things in some places, it had not quite reached where he was living when he was growing up. His world drastically changed when his family moved to Southern California. He found more languages, skin tones, and perspectives than he could have ever imagined. After seminary, Allen took a pastorate in Alabama. He noticed the churches and pastoral gatherings were segmented not just by denomination, but also by ethnicity, gender, and social class. Like in California, the community around him was growing in ethnic diversity. But the churches were not. Allen's theology and ministry practice collided. He wanted his church to reach its ever-growing multi-ethnic community. He felt Scripture did not give him a pass to exclude those who were ethnically different. He wanted his church actively engaged in our globalized society. Allen and others like him are running ahead of most of evangelicalism, and we need to catch up. How are you going to represent Christ amid our globalized society?

TWO BIG CAUTIONS

As you move toward intentionality, keep two big cautions in mind.

Extremes

The first caution is that the days where we can make broad assumptions about people strictly because of their race are gone. As we discussed earlier, race is just now one of many different lenses people use to view the world. Ethnic borders exist all the time, but how important they are is totally based on the individual because of our globalized moment.

In today's world, we can't assume people's ethnicity is the primary way they choose to view their lives. Race is always an influencer because of the society we live in, but as I mentioned in chapter 1, how much it does so is up to the individual. Every person navigates being a representative of his or her identity within the larger society. The following graphic illustrates how this plays out concerning ethnicity.

Ethnic Representative and Advocate Types[2]

Representative Negative	Representative Positive	Advocate Positive	Advocate Negative
Ignores fixity and fluidity of identity Can require one to "choose" an aspect of identity Appearance may not match experience or ethnicity Representative can experience marginalization by inclusion or "token" experience Can be seen as having selfish motives Participates in the "my rights" model that is characteristic of secular thought Rehearses injustices, even if accurate, that can foster bitterness and anger and stall the process of forgiveness Can increase representatives' feeling of isolation and disunity within the community	Can speak passionately and from a place of credibility Not motivated by selfish ambition but forgiveness, love, and unity in the body of Christ Focused on truth, fostering understanding that can lead to positive change within the community As representative, serves as a positive role model Healthy representation, recognizing the need to not overwhelm others with excessive sorrow Integrity in representing subgroup concerns, not personal perspective alone Reflects the character and purpose of Christ	Focuses the Christian's attention on loving the ethnic other Can demonstrate the truth of the situation as true for all as opposed to true for some Free from objections of selfish ambition and can minimize marginalization by inclusion Guards against tendency to disengage or reject own identity Serves as evangelistic testimony to the world of the unity possible in the body of Christ to serve and lift up the needs and concerns of others rather than self	Does not speak with perceived credibility Can put unnecessary burden on people to constantly speak out on the one aspect of identity Can easily be discounted from the "realities on the ground" and unaware of what is primarily helpful Equalizing attempts can introduce new kinds of injustice, further exasperating the relationship dynamic Is unaware of own identity and role of representation Can develop unhealthy guilt issues and reject identity Others can become frustrated by them and disengage

Because of this, we have to be very careful about hires made in the name of diversity. We want representative and advocate positive types. One time after presenting a workshop on reconciliation, Jerome (not his real name), an African-American came up to talk to me. He said he was so grateful for my presentation. He worked for a Christian organization that hired him in the name of ethnic diversity and expected him to bring the racial perspective of the *entire* black community into the ministry. Besides the inability of any one person on the planet to do that, his main problem was that the lens of race was not the primary way he viewed life. In fact, being black was pretty much a footnote for him.

He wasn't ashamed of his blackness, but he had grown up in an extremely multi-ethnic context where people identified themselves through other cultural characteristics (neighborhood, language spoken, economic class, musical tastes, etc.). Race just wasn't that big a deal to him. So he had no knowledge of the race-based "black experience" his organization expected him to bring. His dilemma was that he was a black man without the traditional black experience and really wasn't connected to the consciousness of the overall black community. He really did not possess the skill set to be a bridge builder, and he struggled with what to do about the situation.

Jerome became an innocent participant caught in what I call the "rent-a-race" syndrome. Because it is now in style to be concerned about being multi-ethnic, organizations are more open to hiring people of different ethnicities. They take intentional steps, and this is a good thing. However, do not make the assumption that just because someone is a person of color they automatically possess the skill set to help your organization make inroads into that particular ethnic community or that they will be organizational change agents. There is a lot more to it than that.

Many ethnics are very comfortable being completely assimilated into the dominant group's way of doing things. I will not condemn people who make that choice, but don't make the mistake of thinking people who bring this mind-set to the table will help you make great strides toward ethnic diversity. Assimilation should not be the goal.

On the other end of the spectrum, some people of color are very comfortable with always dropping the hammer. I call them zealots, meaning people who are obsessive and hard-nosed in their quests. They react to white ethnocentrism by becoming ethnocentric themselves. I don't criticize that stance either.

In some cases, it is needed to move the organization along. In fact, if I am completely honest, at times I am very drawn to being one myself! But I resist because I realize that being a zealot most of the time is not very fruitful. We need a whole tool belt, not just a hammer.

And don't make the mistake of thinking zealots only come as people of color. Surprisingly, I have come across more white zealots when it comes to ethnic diversity. I would imagine that is because most ethnic zealots don't last too long in white organizations. They either leave on their own accord or are eventually shown the door.

I've been in situations where the biggest obstacle blocking the integration efforts was the white people who stood for it. It was great that in their zeal they brought attention to problems. But they did more harm than good, because they alienated everyone around them with their insistence that other whites get it—immediately. It's like they figured things out and forgot that they didn't get it overnight.

Grace seems to be nonexistent, but dumping guilt is abundant. The white zealot has an intense need to make all other whites feel guilty for being white, which is kind of odd, being that they are white themselves. Just like I am fine in my skin, I would hope we would want whites to be fine in theirs. I've actually seen organizations that were very willing to make progress, but because of the white zealots among them, they backed off. Things became too intense.

Zealots are not bridge builders any more than those who are "racially rented." Bridge builders are those who have a hybrid personal identity when it comes to ethnicity. It is important for them to understand and stay attached to the ethnic world they represent, while at the same time providing clear understanding to the ethnic others around them. They are grace-giving rebels against the ethnic status quo. They provide a tempo of change just right for the organizational environment. Most importantly, they pursue multi-ethnicity for the kingdom's sake instead of from a foundation of guilt and condemnation (zealots) or misunderstood duplicity when hiring (racially rented).

Good Goals

The second caution is in the area of goal setting. A number of years ago, I attended a conference on how to bring ethnic diversity to college campuses. In one workshop, I was part of a small group where we were to discuss the frustrations each one of us experienced on our campuses as diversity officers. When comparing notes, it was clear that many of us had the same issues. However, about 75 percent of the participants in my group were angry about their situation. They weren't a little annoyed, but downright hostile!

What it boiled down to is that they went into their integration efforts with enthusiasm, but in the midst of experiencing difficulties, they now felt betrayed. This narrative isn't unfamiliar. I can't tell you how many situations where I have been brought in to consult because everybody started with good intentions in trying to integrate a situation and then the whole project crashed and burned with hurt feelings all around.

To prevent such situations, I think it would be good to borrow a teaching from Larry Crabb of the Christian counseling world. He stresses mastering the art of differentiating between goals and desires. He defines a goal as "an outcome that requires only my cooperation to achieve" and a desire as "an outcome that requires the cooperation of another person to be achieved."[3] For example, a goal is to exercise for thirty minutes three times a week; a desire is for my spouse to exercise with me for thirty minutes three times a week. Crabb's theory is that anger and bitterness seep in when we illegitimately make our desires into goals. If I make my spouse exercising with me a goal and she chooses not to do so, I may get angry at her because she is blocking my goal. This is not fair to her because my desire has now become a demand for her to follow. It is an illegitimate goal.

Additionally, I have set myself up for continual frustration, because I cannot control whether she exercises or not. This is helpful to remember both in setting personal life goals or general organizational goals. But this is a golden rule that must be followed when leading toward ethnic diversity within your situation. We must set ethnic diversity goals that are really goals, not desires that masquerade as goals but are illegitimate.

We hold ourselves accountable to our goals and work toward and pray for our desires. A board of trustees may give their university president a goal of 50 percent of their student body being nonwhite in five years. But that is an illegitimate goal because it is a desire. A legitimate goal would be for them to charge the president to plan and execute an effective admissions strategy toward ethnic students. The university president has control over whether that happens or not.

Ethnic integration of a ministry, campus, or nonprofit is a complex process with many opportunities for misunderstandings. When — not if — strategies and plans fail, the first thing that must be determined is whether it was a goal or desire you were working toward. Figuring that out will go a long way in determining if it truly was a failure or a result of idealistic thinking.

One time, while presenting ethnic diversity goals to the EFCA board of directors, I received pushback. Essentially, many of them were saying I was setting the bar too low. They then offered suggestions they felt like I should be shooting for. I had to explain to them that what they were asking for were desires and not goals. I encouraged them to pray toward those lofty expectations they wanted to achieve but to realize they were desires only God could fulfill. I told them that the entire set of goals I was pursuing would have to be achieved prior to their desires for the EFCA coming to pass.

Once we become intentional, we get excited. We realize we need to address issues in a way that involves the perspectives of all ethnicities. However, let me issue a slight note of caution. To use a football analogy, don't outkick your punt coverage. Different life experience gives us different perspectives on racialization. These differences can be addressed, but they have to be engaged correctly. Godly character must abound. The job as leader is to show patience, provide clarity, and give encouragement. If you do these things, most people will respond with humility, listening, and a willingness to learn.

As a leader, you need to know your organization's ethnic story. It's the principle of going back to the past in order to determine your future. The past is still alive for better or worse. You must intentionally engage the legacy that has been passed down to you.

NOTES

1. Chart adapted from Randall B. Lindsey, Kikanza J. Nuri Robins, and Raymond D. Terrell, eds., *Cultural Proficiency: A Manual for School Leaders* (Thousand Oaks, Calif.: Corwin, 1990), 77.

2. Chart adapted from unpublished material developed by Felix and Esther Theonugraha.

3. Larry Crabb, *How to Deal with Anger* (Grand Rapids, Mich.: Zondervan, 1982), 8–12.

SHIFTING TOWARD MULTI-ETHNICITY

PART TWO

SUSTAINABLE
PERFORMANCE

With this chapter, we will transition into creating an organizational response to the three challenges of the first three chapters from the perspective of being a decision-maker. I once heard of a Christian organization that had an issue facing its leadership board involving ethnic conflict. The organization was dominated by two ethnic groups. One was convinced the other was playing favorites toward their "own kind" with one of the programs offered. Not being bashful, they confronted the board with their accusations. What did the board do?

The leadership sat down with those who felt slighted. After hearing their concerns, they prayerfully considered and made changes to the program.

They even went as far as implementing what some might consider affirmative action, expanding the leadership board to include new leaders, all of them coming from the ethnicity of the offended group. It turned out to be win-win for all involved, and the organization thrived. You are probably familiar with the story, because it's the account of the appointing of the first deacons found in Acts 6:1–7.

This passage of Scripture has played a special role in my life. It is a model of how to minister in a globalized world. As I mentioned in the introduction, in the third year of my church-planting experience, I was ready to quit. We had a mass exodus along racial lines. After several heart-to-heart talks with the remaining members, while trying to figure out next steps, Acts 6:1–7 came alive to me. If you are not familiar with it, please make yourself well acquainted, as I find it very helpful to serve as a compass for multi-ethnic leadership.

Here's the background of the text. The Grecian Jews were Jews not native to Palestine who had relocated to Jerusalem. It was considered to be honorable to spend your last days in Jerusalem and to be buried there upon death. Because of this belief, Jews of many different ethnicities from all over the Roman Empire moved there toward the end of their lives. This created a large population of widows.

The Jewish faith took the responsibility of caring for widows as a serious task. Because of the significant amount of nonnative widows located in Jerusalem, it created a social problem. There were not enough foreign Jewish synagogues to keep up with the demands of care. Caring for them was not a value among pagan nonnatives. With no relatives around, the widows were in dire straits. Like racialization, it was a societal problem that leaked into the walls of the church.

If we take the high road, we can assume the Grecian widows were not intentionally discriminated against. There is a high probability the Grecian church widows were not being adequately served simply because of the sheer number of them. But we can't lose sight of human nature and ethnic borders.

Many scholars think that Hebraic Jews, because of ethnic bias, looked down on Grecian Jews, and so there is a strong probability that Grecian widows were intentionally overlooked. The results are the same regardless of motive. A biblical mandate to care for widows was being violated. This text will be a constant reference as we examine different principles.

THE PROBLEM

Maybe the most common problem I've seen among leaders with good multi-ethnic intentions is the inability to deliver sustainable performance in the area of ethnic diversity. Results are typically very uneven. I call it the "dandelion effect." Every spring, like clockwork, my lawn becomes speckled with dandelions. These weeds pop up quickly and spread contagiously. But they don't stick around. After a few weeks, they naturally go away. Such is the case with many multi-ethnic efforts.

Typically, the energy for these efforts lasts anywhere from one to five years, then it is back to status quo. Like dandelions that pop up on a lawn every spring, leaders dream big and hope to have discovered the magic bullet to solve the ethnic diversity issue. Then after a period of time, the initiatives have either died or soured people on the whole idea. When someone new comes on the scene and pitches diversity, the organizational veterans roll their eyes and respond with, "We tried that and it didn't work."

The pattern goes something like this. An organizational desire arises to either start or advance the process of becoming multi-ethnic. Task forces and committees are formed and meetings happen, producing a vision of some sort. This vision of what could be is predominant and the major driving force. Out of this vision, vibrant new relationships are born for the purpose of collaboration to carry out the vision. Moves are made, such as hiring new employees, changing policies, or developing interdependent partnerships with other organizations. Sometimes departments within the organization that traditionally have not worked together begin to do so. This leads to a frenzy of ideas for multi-ethnic innovation.

A lot of creative energy is spent. The by-product is the management of new programs or the reformation of older ones. But the

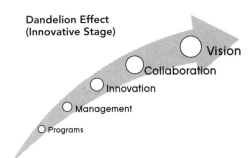

**Dandelion Effect
(Innovative Stage)**

Vision
Collaboration
Innovation
Management
Programs

programs are not the focus. The will for the management of the programs is driven by vision, collaboration, and innovation. Like in Acts 6, problem solving of presenting issues operates at a high level.

In most cases, the beginning of the innovation stage is an exciting time and all is well. There may be pushback, but it is easily pushed through. But then the whole process becomes stagnant. At some point, the multi-ethnic task becomes somewhat of a burden. Pushback increases on whether or not ethnic diversity is worth all the hassle it seems to bring the organization.

The turning point into stagnation is marked usually by one of three factors or some combination of them: (1) all the "low-hanging fruit" has been picked; (2) enough of the original architects of the vision have left, leaving vision amnesia; or (3) major issues arise that no one has a clear answer for or the will to solve them. The programs then become a flashpoint for organizational politics. The will to manage programming wanes. The innovational energy of the creative stage has now morphed into bureaucratic inertia. What used to be vibrant relationships of collaboration have now become silos of isolation, where the goal is to dig in and protect turf and resources. And the vision is off in a galaxy far, far away.

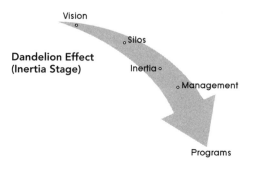

Like the dandelion, the whole multi-ethnic push then just goes away. If programs remain, they are lifeless and only act as placeholders to check the multi-ethnic box on somebody's report. Multi-ethnicity was good for a season, but now it's not a priority.

THE PEOPLE

The biggest variable of whether you can keep the organization in the innovation stage is the people who make up your organization. Author Jim Collins in his book *Good to Great* offers this guiding principle: "First who, then what." He believes those who build great organizations make sure they have the right people on the bus, the wrong people off the bus, and the right people in the key seats *before* they figure out where to drive the bus. They always think first about who and then about what.[1] Some organizational tasks anybody can lead. Such is not the case with ethnic diversity.

The graphic below is a combination of my practical experience and the general rate of the diffusion of innovation. It is my observation that you will have at least five general camps of worldviews on multi-ethnicity at all times within your organization. These are not hard-and-fast categories but more what scholars call "ideal types." I am mainly sharing this knowledge to give you a sense of the worldviews you will face. There are surely exceptions, and people migrate between camps based on the presenting issue at hand.

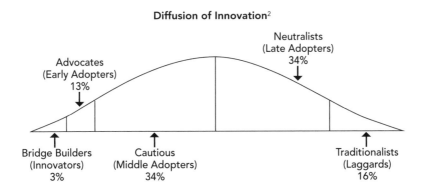

Diffusion of Innovation[2]

Bridge Builders (Innovators, 3 percent)

I would guess a good portion of you reading this book are in this camp. Borrowing a term from the psychology world (which I will do for each camp) we can categorize this group as "unconsciously competent." People in this group have had so much experience with diversity that navigating the dynamics of difference has become second nature. At times they may even wonder why it so hard for others to get it.

People in this camp have an innate ability and desire to reconcile racialization, theology, and the founding DNA in very practical ways. They see ethnic differences as an opportunity to improve the organization. They can be seen as the opposite of the traditionalist group (more on this group later). A flaw is that this group tends to be too idealistic at times. Because of this, they run the risk of becoming fatigued by the whole situation.

These people are trendsetters and reformers. They are the ones who will dream up the new ideas and the direction to take things and serve as thought leaders on the subject. Whether you asked them or not, multi-ethnicity would be a part of their lives, and they are passionate about the subject. It might even be described as a calling. They almost always have significant relationships and life experience across racial lines. They are the people who will provide the most technical help as you figure out how to successfully implement multi-ethnicity within the organization.

Advocates (Early Adopters, 13 percent)

Given that you are reading this book, if you are not a bridge builder, you are probably an advocate. These are people who demonstrate a strong desire to see their organizations be more ethnically inclusive places. They love the organizations and see the opportunities that ethnic diversity brings. They constantly express concern for nonwhites not being welcomed as well as frustration with the pace of organizational change.

These folks often are "consciously incompetent." They are conscious of the fact that something has to change and are not shy about trying to change things. However, because they do not possess the experience of bridge builders, in their eagerness they often offend the very ones they are trying to lead, which at times makes them incompetent. They make many mistakes of the heart that often turn out to be great occasions for organizational learning.

They are important because other camps look to this group for guidance and knowledge about multi-ethnic initiatives. They gain the reputation as the "safe" people to talk about potentially divisive issues. In the end, this group serves as a role model for those who are trying to make a decision whether or not to get on board. Their stamp of approval is what sparks critical mass acceptance.

Cautious (Middle Adopters, 34 percent)

This actually may be the most important group, because they link together those who get it early on with those who get it later. Because of their role and the size of the group, they make or break an organization's efforts. One word for this group is *deliberate*. They won't be the first on board, but they will not be the last to sign on either.

These people are "consciously competent." They know how to get things done in their organization. They are tremendous team players. They "get it" concerning ethnic diversity but proceed with caution. They are concerned with making sure that embracing multi-ethnicity is biblical, and they also serve as the guardians of what they perceive to be violations of the founding DNA—if things change too quickly to accommodate multi-ethnicity.

The cautious play a pivotal role in keeping an organization's efforts connected to important organizational DNA and theological tenets of the faith. But if they are unconvinced, these people can use this position as a bully pulpit to block progress. Multi-ethnic efforts die on the vine from paralysis by analysis.

This group comes aboard right before the idea goes viral, and they are probably not very vocal about their opinions. You can tell by their actions that they are in agreement, but they will seldom lead the effort. They frequently interact with people in each camp and serve as the glue that makes multi-ethnicity stick.

Neutralists (Late Adopters, 34 percent)

These are people who demonstrate a need to not consider the role of race in any particular situation. They go to the trainings and read all the books, but they always play a constant drumbeat, challenging whether race plays a pivotal role in the situation at hand. Other variables are always brought into the conversation to lessen the weight race may play in a particular situation.

Although they are "unconsciously incompetent" because they struggle with valuing ethnic diversity, they will play ball mainly because of the cautious group. Neutralists might not be totally for it, but they aren't necessarily against it either. They will go along to get along, but they won't do so until leadership and colleague peer pressure makes it a necessity.

Traditionalists (Laggards, 16 percent)

This is the "legacy lobby." These are people demonstrating a pattern of not being able to discern the practical individual and institutional implications of racialization or the present historical moment. They just can't make sense of it all. The consciousness here is complacency. Leaders should take the high road with these people. Even in their struggle with understanding, traditionalists may still adopt, but it will just take them much longer.

Their biggest problem is that the past means so much to them that they just can't let it go. They pretty much run *all* organizational decisions based on what was done in the past, because to them, that is the way forward. Leaders must be careful not to make traditionalists scapegoats for holding up progress. They are small in number, and if 16 percent of the people can hold up 84 percent of the others, it indicates a huge problem in how decisions are made in the organization.

Leading toward God's multi-ethnic kingdom is more art than science, and battles should be chosen wisely. In light of these camps, I have a few guidelines for leading:

- Overall, focus on bringing out the best and curtailing the worst. It is the only way you can lead all of these camps together in unity.
- Provide as many opportunities as possible for bridge builders and advocates.

- Provide as many resources as possible for the cautious, so they can understand the purpose and need for the changes.
- Provide the same for the neutralists, as they take additional time to consider the changes. Be patient because when critical mass happens, they will come on board.
- Provide motivation for the traditionalists. If they hold major decision-making power, they may need to prayerfully consider moving on, or you may have to lessen their responsibilities so they will not be a roadblock.

DEALING WITH PRESENTING ISSUES

The leadership in Acts 6:1–7 modeled how to engage presenting issues. The response was not to be blind to ethnic bias charges, blame the offended ethnic group with causing trouble, or eliminate the concern as the "social gospel." They went to work, and we should follow their lead. I call organizations that display certain traits "Acts 6 organizations." Here are some general characteristics of these types of institutions.

They Embrace Ethnic Diversity as an Organizational DNA Adventure (vv. 1–2)

When we intend to do something monumental, such as build a new state-of-the-art building or hire a new president, strategic planning is involved. On certain issues, we know every department and organizational stakeholder will be affected. I call those "organizational DNA adventures." We develop long-term plans for things we expect to stick.

On these types of ventures, we stress "all hands on deck" and spend a lot of time tracking progress and strategizing how we can get better. So I am continually amazed by the blank stares I get from people when I ask, "What is your long-term organizational plan for ethnic diversity?" Often there is no coherent, rational blueprint readily available.

Failing to rationally plan a strategy guarantees the dandelion effect. I talked in chapter 1 about how leaders have to make ethnic journeys of understanding a part of their lifestyle. It's the same on the institutional level. Your organization has to be on a corporate journey of expanding its ethnic learning. It can't be done unless it is planned out. This systematic, intentional planning is what makes ethnic diversity a part of your organizational DNA.

Every organization has a range of topics to be addressed. Some are simple, like symbolically projecting that you value diversity through pictures on your website or the artwork on your walls. Others are more difficult like changing a bylaw that has been around for eighty years. These topics will never be addressed unless they are systematically engaged.

They Leverage Ethnic Difference (vv. 3–4)

Another question I ask that brings blank stares is, "Why should this organization be multi-ethnic?" It will never be part of the organizational DNA if you cannot thoroughly answer this question. Answering this in a way that brings unity is not a slam dunk.

Remember that the challenges of ethnic borders, racialization, and unintentionality will provide reservoirs of resistance to the reasoning that ethnic diversity is important for organizational success. People live in psychic prisons, and your role will be to set them free. Because of this, as I stated earlier, your diversity-specific programming will become a flashpoint.

You must create multiple spaces of active learning where racial perceptions can be modified. That is deeply personal work, and care must be taken that such work is done by skilled facilitators of learning. It also means providing lanes for people to run in and helping them decide the direction to run. By being consistent in reinforcing the value of ethnic diversity, you will improve the chances of people helping instead of hurting the multi-ethnic change process.

They Mobilize Money and Personnel toward Solutions (vv. 5–6)

Only a select few Christian organizations can operate under the premise that money is no problem. The reality for most of us is that we have a limited financial pool to accomplish many important tasks.

There are often more good ideas than money to fund them in any given year. But we fund what we prioritize. The reality is that if you are going to be serious about this, it is probably going to require a reallocation of resources or focused fund-raising for expansion. I've heard many leaders say, "We'll get around to it once we have the money." It is a stalling tactic, unless the next sentence is a plan on how to get the money and a hard deadline as to when the idea will be funded.

The other issue tied at the hip with money is personnel. I've heard criticism of the creation of my position at the EFCA because diversity "should be everybody's job, not just one man." People who lob such criticisms obviously have no idea what my job entails. We have around fourteen hundred churches in the United States and eighty-five national office personnel. I wouldn't get very far if it all fell on me to do everything. But things labeled "everybody's job" have a tendency to be nobody's job. What I do is provide primary leadership to what we call our "all people" strategy. Every organization needs a primary leader on the "C" level of the organization chart to spearhead ethnic diversity efforts. In some places, it may make sense to bring in a chief diversity officer (CDO). A CDO is an emerging position, particularly in the business and university worlds, and is what my position is modeled after.

My role has emerged in order to build EFCA ethnic diversity capacity within the context of our globalized society, particularly among our churches in the US. In the EFCA, ethnic diversity is not an end goal, accomplishment, experience, or plan. The vision is to create a network of churches that defines reconciliation as the mission of God in our fallen world.

This means we have to train our church leaders how to engage race, social class, gender, disability, and other societal divisions. We want our church leaders to stress both proclamation and demonstration of the gospel. In short, I am here to help the EFCA become the best denomination in the world that lives out the Great Commandments in order to fulfill the Great Commission.

At both my positions at Cincinnati Christian University and the EFCA, I started out as a part-time, one man shop. I am now full-time with the EFCA. Both of those organizations are much further down the road concerning sustainable performance because they brought in a point person to oversee their ethnic diversity efforts. If you are willing to reallocate money to do the same, I predict you will see much better results with your organization as well.

In some instances, it might not make sense to do so, like in a church setting or if your organization is not large enough to justify a CDO. But don't drop the responsibility of providing point leadership on the issue. I would recommend giving the task to someone on the senior leadership team who has passion and is a bridge builder or advocate in this area. Give away some of their other responsibilities to others so they can spend time leading integration efforts.

They Provide Clarity (v. 7)

Because of the myriad of perspectives brought to the table regarding multi-ethnicity, at times it's difficult to project a clear vision. So we tend to stay on the surface of this crucial topic unaware of the assumptions we are making. Unity might be as simple as thoroughly defining the objective. When engaging in issues with ethnic subtexts, the single most important thing is to be crystal clear about what the issue at hand is. I've seen many disconnects where one party is talking about one thing and the other is talking about something totally different. But they think they are discussing the same thing.

Within the EFCA, we decided to define our diversity efforts under the broader term *reconciliation*. Over the years, I have figured out that when I say *reconciliation*, some common things people hear are:

- Peacemaking
- Social gospel
- Social justice
- Blacks and whites getting along
- Cultural diversity
- Universalism
- Liberalism
- Democratic party supporter
- Political correctness

But when I say *reconciliation*, I don't mean any of these. So I have learned that you cannot spend enough time defining terms in order for maximum clarity to be achieved. Once you have, earnest dialogue can begin. Whatever term you decide to utilize with your constituency to impart the vision, make sure to define it relentlessly.

As a reminder, it is also important that you continuously define it as an organizational value instead of something to be achieved. It's about more than political correctness or the number of people in the pews or classroom. When it is a value, you weather the ups and downs and press on.

No matter what happens, your organization will always value certain things. You know what they are. You may even jokingly refer to them as sacred cows. Some of them are legitimate and some are not, but they are deeply held values that will not go quietly into the night if someone tries to remove them. If you are going to lead toward God's multi-ethnic kingdom, ethnic diversity must be clearly communicated as one of those key values.

THE PATH

Too many times when leaders go down the path of leading ethnic diversity, the call is to be radical. Being radical only works in the midst of a revolution. It is negatively focused on tearing down things and is deficit based. Unless your organization is in the midst of a crisis, being radical is not going to work. Wise leaders know you don't throw out the proverbial baby with the bathwater. In Acts 6, the people followed a pattern of being inside out, top down, and all in.

Make no mistake about the fact that you are a change agent. And you know what they say about change: People love it as long as it is not happening to them. Those who worship at the altar of the past constantly rev their engines and accelerate in reverse, thinking they are in drive. Those who love change for change's sake floor it while in drive, rapidly racing toward instability. If you are not careful, your organization will be in the middle between the two factions, and no one wins in that scenario.

Change has a rhythm to it based on where the organization is. If change is not properly introduced, it will quickly turn to chaos. And wherever your organization is, if you come from a place of strength (assets), you stand a much better chance of moving forward. To stay sharp, always look for ways to prevent the dandelion effect. To prevent the weeds from spreading, you must be vigilant to stay in the innovation stage.

Keeping the organization in the innovation stage keeps the focus on unearthing assets to utilize toward the multi-ethnic task. The vision has to stay at the forefront; collaboration must be encouraged; innovation is a must; and proper resources need to be provided for program management. Embrace the task as a phenomenal leadership opportunity.

As the Lord moved me from the pastorate to working with Christian organizations to develop ethnic diversity, I let my moral imagination flow. What would it look like for our organizations to bring about the changes necessary? How can we go about making all things new, as Scripture declares (see 2 Cor. 5:17)? I think I have found some key insights into what works.

In the late 1990s, I came across a wonderful book entitled *Building Communities from the Inside Out* by John Kretzmann and John McKnight.[3] It serves to guide those interested in urban community development and provide ways to go about it. Typically, urban areas are deemed inherently deficient. The glass is seen as half empty, so to speak. Of course, another view is to look at the glass as half full. But why focus on whether the glass is half full or half empty? The problem is that the glass doesn't have enough liquid in it! The real question is, "How do we raise the level in the glass?" So don't focus primarily on the needs and deficiencies of a community, but rather the capacities and gifts of the community and the people who live within it.

Kretzmann and McKnight claim that this posture is a more effective approach to developing an urban community, and I wholeheartedly agree. I followed their blueprint while I served as an urban pastor and saw wonderful results. I am officially hooked by the idea of operating from an asset-based foundation.

Don't focus on the needs and racial deficiencies. Everybody who wants to know pretty much knows there are problems. On the other hand, this doesn't mean you should ignore them. I always tell people I supervise, "Don't bring me a problem unless you have a suggestion for a solution." The constant pointing out of ethnic problems without offering potential corresponding correctives is called whining. Instead, the focus should be on releasing the capacities and gifts of your employees and the organization. As you do this, you will address the deficiencies and needs, raising the liquid level in the glass so to speak. This type of philosophy I define as "asset-based diversity development." It can be summed up with a phrase that I have already mentioned: inside out, top down, and all in.

Inside Out

The most significant change occurs from the inside out. The people who have the most to lose and the most to gain from developing ethnic diversity in your organization are those who work for you. What you need is an intentional process to unleash the talents of these critical stakeholders. Significant diversity development only takes place when those who care most about the organization are committed to bringing it to pass.

Every single organization boasts a distinctive mixture of people who can help build a preferred multi-ethnic future. Your task is to organize their gifts, skills, and capacities to shoot toward the same target. When making use of these assets, welcome the Holy Spirit to unlock an infinite collection of personal gifts and fruitful skills among those you lead.

One time, while working with a well-known parachurch ministry, I was hit with a barrage of questions. I told them to meet me the next week for a meeting, and I would bring somebody in that would tremendously help them. The next week I brought in one of their few ethnic employees and said, "Ask him what you asked me last week." They were amazed by what they learned.

This doesn't mean that you should never seek outside help in leading toward diversity. The question of where change comes from—inside or outside—does not have an either/or answer, but a both/and answer. By "inside out," I don't mean you have all the answers within the organization. At times it is strategic to bring in outside voices to hear their perspectives. (I will talk more about this in chapter 6.) But you will always gain the most by motivating and facilitating contributions from those who know the organization most intimately.

The more people of color you have who are passionate about your organization and connected to the values of their ethnic community, the better. They will serve as the best catalysts to raise your organizational consciousness about what needs to be done internally.

Some of you are at ground zero with ethnic employees. If you have little diversity, getting some ethnic staff members on the payroll who understand your foundational DNA is a good place to start. Put as many resources as possible to integrate at least 20 percent of your workforce with the "ethnic other." In fact, at least 20 percent is a good marker to use for your boards and senior leadership too. Research has shown that 20 percent is a critical mass for raising the multi-ethnic consciousness across the whole of the Christian organization.[4] It is the beginning point of true integration.

Top Down

Another significant variable for sustainable performance regarding multi-ethnic diversity is whether major decision-makers embrace or refuse to embrace ethnic diversity. Key leaders in key positions will directly affect your ability to sustain multi-ethnic efforts. Your ability to operate as a change agent is exponentially increased if the people around you — the ones who make things go — share a preferred future for the organization in this area.

Although the grassroots of the organization is important, if anything of significance is going to be accomplished, it will be because the main decision-makers are contributing their time, energy, and resources. The power of change is unleashed when individuals with authority have a common vision. If we go back to the innovation stage graphic (dandelion effect), the higher up on the organization chart the process happens the broader the impact. The reality is that until the senior leadership embraces the direction, ethnic diversity will remain on an island of good intentions.

All In

The top of the organizational chart has to drive change, but the grassroots employees play a significant role. Like I demonstrated with inside out, leaders have to be willing to contribute their talents and gifts to the cause. And since there are more employees than senior leaders, collectively, they make the final decision whether any significant change is going to take place.

Therefore, it is imperative that we have built-in evaluative systems that surface where people stand on this issue. I have found that as much as you try to bring in the right people who have a multi-ethnic-friendly attitude, in the globalized moment we live in, most have figured out the right thing to say in an interview. You really don't know until the person is in the midst of doing the job where they really stand.

One thing to do is build a systemic learning system around ethnic issues. Seminars, workshops, and e-learning tools are not magic bullets, but they can be important spaces where you will unearth values, attitudes, and beliefs. Another is to put valuing diversity in the general responsibilities of every employee and incorporate it in your employee evaluation reviews. Doing these simple steps signals that the organization is serious about ethnic diversity.

Inside out, top down, and all in is the philosophy to carry forward. The process that accompanies the asset-based philosophy is one that: (1) is Word-based and Spirit-filled; (2) is team and transformative in

nature; and (3) has accountable alignment. This will produce a ripple effect. The next few chapters will guide you on the process.

NOTES

1. Jim Collins, *Good to Great: Why Some Companies Make the Leap . . . and Others Don't* (New York: HarperCollins, 2001), 41.

2. Graphic (with slight modifications) from Everett Rogers, *Diffusion of Innovations* (New York: Simon & Schuster, 2003), Kindle edition, 5865.

3. John P. Kretzmann and John L. McKnight, *Building Communities from the Inside Out: A Path toward Finding and Mobilizing a Community's Assets* (Chicago: ACTA Publications, 1993).

4. This is the standard used by leading sociologists who study racial integration and religious organizations. See the work by Curtiss Paul DeYoung et al., *United by Faith: The Multi-Racial Congregation as an Answer to the Problem of Race* (Oxford: Oxford University Press, 2003); and Brad Christerson, Korie L. Edwards, and Michael O. Emerson, *Against All Odds: The Struggle for Racial Integration in Religious Organizations* (New York: New York University Press, 2005).

MULTI-ETHNIC CHANGE AS SPIRITUAL GROWTH

Have you ever seen a big rock splash into a lake? Ripples flow out from the center, resonating across the surface in flaring circles. Or how about a steady rain on a pond, where the raindrops create individual ripples that together create an event of hundreds of circles, radiating out on the surface, rippling across the water?

By focusing inside out, top down, and all in, the goal is to create such a ripple effect in your organization. In this chapter, we will deal with the catalyzing splash that will generate the energy for the circles to ripple across the organization. It begins with a shift from a secular perspective of racial tolerance to a spiritual core of having a strong, biblical apologetic, connecting your founding DNA and welcoming the Holy Spirit as the foundation of your efforts.

My past experience tells me this chapter will be the one that turns on the light bulb for many of you. It's not that you didn't understand the previous chapters, but many people have said that the content in this chapter was the turning point for them in gaining a deep understanding of the asset-based philosophy.

I have surmised that the reason is because of people's preconceived notions about leading toward multi-ethnicity. They thought they were in for another celebration of racial tolerance. They had been there and done that at a secular place of employment or in a college class. But the distinction between racial tolerance and racial transcendence clarified for them the significance of pursuing ethnic diversity.

CLARIFYING THE CORE

I believe we are at the beginning of a broad rippling of emerging new ideas on how we can effectively operate in a multi-ethnic, globalized world. We all know Martin Luther King, Jr. said the famous quote that "11:00 on Sunday morning remains the nation's most segregated hour." Similar sentiments can be used to describe Christian universities and nonprofits as well. Overwhelmingly, our organizations are still racially homogeneous.

Growing Racial Tolerance

However, there is research showing this may be changing, even if ever so slightly. Because of our globalized moment, we may have the best opportunity ever afforded us to break out of this rut. Robert Putnam and David Campbell's research in *American Grace* (particularly chapter 9, "Diversity, Ethnicity, and Religion") demonstrates the link between religion and race within the US.[1] The data shows a clear correlation between ethnicity and church congregations and denominations, indicating how they are interdependent of each other. I believe this to be true for Christian universities and nonprofits as well. Essentially, their research summation is that after decades of having the least tolerant racial attitudes, evangelicals are now virtually indistinguishable from the rest of the population when it comes to racial attitudes.

Putnam and Campbell make the case that evangelicals have simply followed the national trends—never leading, always following, and now finally catching up. This is a plus. It's the farthest the American church has ever been concerning racial attitudes. But we need to operate very strategically in our globalized historical moment, because although it is a strength, it also has a shadow side. Every strong point brings with it potential danger, a shadow side that unless managed will either inadvertently dilute the strong point or turn it into a hindrance. When it comes to multi-ethnicity, if a leader doesn't pay attention to the subtle nuances of racial tolerance, it could derail his or her efforts.

One of the popular and esteemed ideas of our secular society is supporting ethnic diversity. Racial tolerance (permissive attitudes toward those who are racially different from you) is in style, as Putnam and Campbell's research points out. In a global village of intensifying wars over ethnic identity and difference, many are on a quest, seeking a way to stay united. With the rise of worldwide immigration, many who were considered strangers from a foreign land are now the neighbor from whom we borrow a lawnmower. Society needs a way to exist together, and tolerance is the way we've chosen.

You will be hard-pressed to find an institution (outside of religious ones) that does not offer training on racial diversity. In fact, most public universities even have a center promoting multiculturalism and offering degrees like African-American, Latino, or Asian studies. Corporations have been operating with diversity as a corporate value for decades. Ethnic diversity is not just acknowledged but applauded with enthusiasm.

There are great aspects to living in a time such as this. For one thing, ethnic difference can be leveraged like never before. Our unique backgrounds make the world a little more exciting to live in. And what a privilege that, unlike my father, I have not really had any Mount-Everest-sized barriers put in my way by society to achieve my life goals. I would much rather society be racially tolerant than intolerant. I don't ever want it to be acceptable again to be a leader at a church and a member of the KKK, which was the norm in some geographic areas in the not-so-distant past. There are always incidents that are the exception to the rule, but for the most part we seem to be way past such obvious scriptural violations in our institutions.

More times than not, when I talk to twentysomethings, they don't get all the fuss I'm making. There are people in their forties and fifties who don't get it either! But the difference lies in *why* they don't get it. Many people age forty and up don't get it because they are trying to be color-blind. The twentysomethings see color vividly, but it registers differently for them.

Twentysomethings have grown up in a world marked by multiculturalism, diversity, and cultural competence. I spend time on college campuses, and it is rare to run into a student who hasn't gone to several racial tolerance seminars (many sponsored by their high schools) by the time they are eighteen. They also desire to live in mixed racial company. Even if they grew up in a racially segregated community, they turn on their TVs, go to the movies, or log onto social media and are exposed to different nationalities all the time.

The Shadow Side of Racial Tolerance

But there is a shadow side to this atmosphere of racial tolerance. First, there is the threat of developing a false sense of security. "Daddy, when did racism end?" is the question my twelve-year-old asked me the other day.

"What do you mean?" was my response. What she meant to ask was when the civil rights movement occurred. In her (and many others') mind, that pretty much solved everything. Such is the typical attitude of many in the post-civil rights generation.

Second, with all the celebration of difference that goes on, ironically, it can create an environment of self-centered ethnocentrism. It is one thing to acknowledge your ethnicity, but quite another to worship it. Ethnic self-sufficiency has become an idol for some. The stress is on gathering information about people's differences, but this cannot be an endpoint. There is no direct correlation between people having more information about ethnicities and changing moral attitudes.

Third, in a supposed "post-racial" world, claims of racial prejudice or discrimination are easily muted. An instance where race obviously plays a role may be written off as something else: "It must not have been racially motivated, because we're beyond all that." In some instances, this makes the truth extremely hard to reach. We can't examine power dynamics to determine whose ethnic interests are being served, because we can only see them in positive light in a politically correct atmosphere.

Fourth, when something becomes popular, it has a tendency to be taken for granted. When something is taken for granted, it is rarely thought about in a deep way. Popular concepts have that effect. Try this experiment: Go to church and ask a hundred people what grace is, and you'll get a hundred different responses. Most of them will be correct, but many will be way off base on what the Bible says about grace.

This brings me to my fifth and most important point about the shadow side of living in the age of racial tolerance. Ask average Christians why they should racially accept others and you will probably not receive biblical responses. Their answers will typically run along the lines of what their parents taught them, how they feel, résumés of what they have done to demonstrate their love for ethnic others, what they learned in cultural diversity seminars, or what their favorite political media "talking head" said about the issue. If Scripture is cited, it will be an "it's in the Bible somewhere" type of answer. It's true; it is in there. But the problem is people don't know where or what Scripture actually says.

It is commonplace to have spent very little biblical reflection on the matter. During my PhD research project from 2005 to 2006, I talked to Christians at a Christian institution about what they thought about racial reconciliation. Here are the four things I discovered:

- They didn't think it was relevant to their faith, although they thought it was important.
- They only thought in terms of black versus white.
- They didn't think it was critical to the mission of the institution.
- They were not openly against the concept, but not actively for it either.

The responses reflect the common, disjointed view that is out there. On the one hand is the shadow side influence of the racial age of tolerance. On the other hand is biblical illiteracy, meaning that most people lack a basic understanding of how to think biblically about ethnic diversity. These two realities make up the environment of most diversity efforts, and it is problematic.

WHAT'S THE MOTIVATION?

Being Word-based and providing spiritual inspiration are musts for pursuing ethnic diversity. It is the core for the asset-based philosophy. It will be the primary incentive for every idea you ask people to implement. If you do not start here, you are leaving the biggest gifts you have—the Bible and your faith—on the sidelines.

This came into focus my first year on the job with the EFCA. I was fresh from earning my doctorate and eager to share all that I had learned with our leaders. I designed training that was heavy in social analysis and light on theology. On the typical presentation review form, people would express an appreciation for what I was saying but also concern that the presentation was unbiblical.

These responses were baffling to me. I had been a pastor and studied at the denominational seminary. Many had also heard me preach on other topics. With this knowledge, how could people still make such charges? Needless to say, my phone was not ringing off the hook with offers to come and speak to local congregations.

One day a colleague walked into my office. Greg had recently heard one of my presentations and had some suggestions. At first I'll admit I was defensive and thought, "Here we go." But Greg was very kind in his criticism and offered a suggestion that changed the whole trajectory of my ministry within the EFCA.

"Why don't you add a strong theological component to your presentation?" he asked.

"That would be a waste of time," I said. "Everybody knows you are supposed to love your neighbor."

"Yeah, but everybody doesn't know *why* or *how*."

In this brief exchange, my mystery was solved.

In high school, I took a drama class. At times we would be given scenarios to act out. The teacher would always give what he called "motivation" for the scene. *Motivation* in the acting world means the reasoning behind the heart of every scene, to get you in touch with the moment and put you in the right mind-set. By laying out a biblical apologetic for multi-ethnicity, you are providing the motivation for the people you lead to embrace change. Greg was wisely showing me that I was leaving out the motivation.

Toward Racial Transcendence

If we do not give people biblical motivation, they will likely be content with mere racial tolerance. Racial tolerance is needed for our globalized world to work together, but the church is called beyond tolerance. We are called by the Bible to racial transcendence. So our efforts to lead toward multi-ethnicity must have the foundation of being Spirit-filled and Word-based. The endgame of our journey of building multi-ethnic institutions is not tolerance; that is a by-product. Give people the motivation needed to transcend. I have already written in detail about the nations in the biblical narrative (see chapter 1). What I shared is the biblical apologetic for multi-ethnicity that I use with the leaders I train. Feel free to use it as yours.

The Bible insists we have a responsibility to all ethnic groups. People are to learn God's heart via the witness of God's people. It's like the scene given in Isaiah 25, where all people are called to a banquet arranged by God and where the cloak of death will be taken from the faces of everyone (25:6–8). In this passage, all nations celebrate what God has done by responding, "Behold, this is our God; we have waited for him that he might save us. This is the LORD; we have waited for him; let us be glad and rejoice in his salvation" (25:9 ESV). But before Israel accomplished this monumental achievement, they went through a period of trusting other nations for their well-being instead of God. They trusted in the glory of human strength and ingenuity instead of the glory of God.

I am saying to place your trust in God and communicate that intentionally throughout the process. When we trust in human ingenuity, we can't really reach our goal of multi-ethnicity. I've had some great dialogue with fellow Christians about my stance on this. They often make claims that the secular world is ahead of us on this topic. I totally disagree that the grass is greener on the other side—the grass is green where you water it. Sure there are great corporate, educational, and governmental antiracism programs. We can, as the saying goes, "eat the meat and throw away the bones" from these programs. But what's the motivation for these programs? Often it is financial profit or a legal requirement to pursue multi-ethnicity. Some may have a moral motive, but often their moral foundation is based more in a humanistic universalism than Christianity. You have to have a clear foundation.

Social analysis, peace studies, and other non-Christian tools have their place. They can aid us because truth is truth wherever it is found. I am urging you to not make it your core motivator for change in your organization. It will only take you so far and will betray you in the end. It is an end all unto itself. Pursuing only tolerance is not trustworthy because the motivation does not emanate from a godly perspective.

Tiers of Multi-Ethnicity

The graphic below illustrates the tiers of multi-ethnicity in an organization. The first three tiers are either endpoints or phases of development, depending on the situation. Whether you get to the fourth tier is totally dependent on your core and what your main motivation is.

Tiers of Integrated Organizations

Reconciliation
Motivation: Biblical
Organizational Culture: Multi-Ethnic

Toleration
Motivation: Legal, Profit, or Moral
Organizational Culture: Mixed-Color

Assimilation
Motivation: Legal or Profit
Organizational Culture: Multicolor

Segregation
Motivation: None
Organizational Culture: Homogeneous

The first tier is segregation, and that speaks for itself.

The second tier is the stage many organizations that claim multi-ethnicity are really at: assimilation. They are multicolored. There may be other ethnic groups present, but their cultural perspective has zero bearing on the opinions, thoughts, or direction of the organization. When you look at the totality of their organizational culture (policies, practices, and procedures), it really only reflects the perspective of the dominating racial group. Those ethnics who stick around are either OK with this arrangement or grin and bear it.

The third tier (toleration) is the stage our globalized society generally aims for: tolerance. This is all about getting along. As I've said before, I am not against this. This is better than assimilation because there are unique and distinctive elements of all races within the organization present in the organizational culture. The organization is mixed-color, indicating progress.

Our desire is to reach the fourth tier: reconciliation. This is where organizational culture is an authentic hybrid of all races represented in the organization. No one dominates the other. Our overarching goal is to have our staffs, boards, faculties, congregants, or students experience deep biblical reflection and practical spiritual application regarding multi-ethnicity in order for them to grow in their faith. It is a corporate act of reconciliation with both God and our broken world. The Christian way to unity is to understand differences and act on commonalities. We are to unify on the common ground of Christ and follow where he leads us.

The Power of Reconciliation

In order for that to occur, we must establish a spiritual sense among the people we lead. We must push them past tolerance. I believe the theological foundation of our efforts is expressed in Scripture as the concept of reconciliation. The Duke Center for Reconciliation has a fantastic definition of how the Bible frames things. "Reconciliation is God's initiative, restoring a broken world to his intentions by reconciling 'to himself all things' through Christ: the relationship between people and God, between people themselves, and with God's created earth. Christians participate with God by being transformed into ambassadors of reconciliation."[2]

When people ask me why the EFCA is pursuing ethnic diversity, I tell them that we desire to establish a culture of people who believe reconciliation is the mission of God in our fallen world. Pursuing that supports a platform for ethnic diversity to thrive. At our core, we desire something way beyond tolerance. It's the biblical call of reconciliation, rooted in our faith in God to be able to transcend the troubles of this world that racialization brings. We veer from the celebration of racial tolerance because we celebrate God's reconciliation resolution for his creation.

There is not any magic program that will get you to where you need to be. Be very cautious of anybody who promises you that. You cannot copy your way to success. The way forward has to be custom-made by God for your unique situation. Of course, you can prepare by doing things like reading this book, but the specific directions of what to do lie in the spiritual life of the leadership.

Creating Space for Spiritual Growth

One of the assumptions of being a leader in a Christian organization is that we have the mature seasoning and outstanding character to represent God's kingdom. Our jobs as leaders are to escort our organizations alongside the will of God. When we have been infected by Scripture, our organizations will also be influenced. Therefore we need to be well-versed practical theologians on the topic of multi-ethnicity. We then need to teach those we lead what the Bible has to say on the matter. Creating learning spaces for people to diligently study the Bible on this topic may seem like overkill in a Christian environment, but it is a key ingredient for keeping traction. It keeps us focused on why we are making multi-ethnic correctives. When problems arise, we can become weary.

There will be many misunderstandings on your quest for multi-ethnicity. Among other things, people may reject your suggestions, accuse you of having a hidden agenda, and even sabotage activities for which you spent months planning. If you don't personally stay in study or keep your organization in devotional mode, bitterness both individually and institutionally may take root. Nothing revives the organizational soul like regular time in God's awe-inspiring Word.

The more in-depth you know what Scripture has to say, the more practical principles you will pick up to apply to situations as they arise. Our example for this kind of work is found in the Pauline Epistles, where Paul applied what he knew about God's mission to specific challenges faced by churches. To lead toward multi-ethnicity, we need to be prepared to do the same thing.

The companion of faithful Scripture study is prayer. Acts 6:1–7 is filled with references to the leaders being dependent on the Holy Spirit to guide them in how to solve the presenting issue. When people realize their leaders are in constant touch with God, they are encouraged to boldly go before the throne of grace themselves. They subconsciously pick up that whatever you are constantly praying for is what is important to the organization. Do you have a regular, organized system of prayer for your multi-ethnic desires? I will go so far to say that, if the answer is no, then you do not have any right to expect anything to happen. Jesus reminded us about the power of prayer in Mark 9:29, where the disciples had failed the task they were given, and Christ told them, "This kind can come out only by prayer."

Our primary role is to do what author Henry Blackaby popularized years ago—to find where God is working and join him there. We play the role of leaders in our organizations, but ultimately the task of multi-ethnicity belongs to God. We are to represent his desires, and there is no doubt he desires for us to be ambassadors of reconciliation (see 2 Cor. 5:14–21). To be effective ambassadors, we need to be in harmony with God. That cannot happen unless we are spending quality time in prayer.

We need to challenge our people to be prayer partners around the change process. By doing so, we are following the pattern of Jesus. Many times he withdrew from the busyness of leading in order to pray. As we do this, we develop the mind of Christ and gain perspective on what critical moves to make. We cannot separate who we are spiritually from the task at hand.

See the multi-ethnic change process you are leading as an opportunity to shepherd people. I know from my pastoral background that the number one thing I could do for my membership when I was pastoring was to pray for them. Successful shepherding, regardless of context, is the result of a large amount of time put in praying not only *for* the people you shepherd, but also *with* them. Some of the most spiritually powerful times I ever experienced as a pastor were in living rooms and by hospital beds, praying with congregants (see Acts 6:6).

A practical example is that I have two prayer teams. One is an inner-circle team. This is a small group that loves me and my family and is committed to my ministry. With this group, I often vent about frustrations of trying to lead multi-ethnicity, and I feel free to share in confidence anything that is going on in my personal life. I communicate with them on a regular basis. I don't know what I would do without them.

I also have a second, larger prayer team of a couple hundred people who are committed to praying for me and the ministry on a monthly basis. I send out a monthly prayer newsletter sharing the progress we are making in the EFCA on reconciliation. Often, right before training events or consultation meetings, using social media, I send them and others brief prayer requests in order to ignite spontaneous prayer. I firmly believe that any success I see is primarily because these two prayer groups undergird my efforts.

I wish I could tell you that I pray for our multi-ethnic efforts every day, but I would be lying. However, I do pray more days during the week than I do not. I am radically committed to taking one day a month to get away for meditation and Bible study and three consecutive days a year for the same thing to kick off the ministry year. During this time, I also practice fasting and ministry planning.

CONNECTING FOUNDING DNA

Leadership in this realm is all about getting people to move in a new direction. Motivation is all about inspiring followers. Besides being Word-based and Spirit-filled, it is an important asset for decision-makers to tie in the organization's founding DNA in some way to your change efforts. The easiest way to do so is to create a story that ties the valuable traditions of the past with the present multi-ethnic direction of the future. This will personify and give greater worth to the change process you are leading.

Stories have tremendous power. Think about how the creation story of Adam and Eve or the crucifixion story is utilized in the Bible to inspire us to go in a certain direction. As a spiritual child of the African-American church, in my tradition, every sermon traditionally ends with "raising him," or tying everything you have taught, regardless of topic, to the resurrection power of Jesus Christ. The goal is for people to leave with an attitude of hope for their situations.

The power of your multi-ethnic story lies in its appeal to your stakeholders and those you want to become a part of your organization. It should have the elements of how you are part of the worldwide Christian movement known as the church, but also how you are distinctive from others in this movement. And it revolves around your organizational role in furthering God's kingdom by pursuing multi-ethnicity.

When the EFCA decided to lead our churches to tackle the topic of immigration, our director of Hispanic ministries (Alejandro Mandes) came up with the following multi-ethnic story:

It can be said that we *all* are immigrants here in America. But not all denominations in America can claim the same deep roots to immigration. The EFCA historical roots are the combination of three Scandinavian peoples coming together in America with a deep heritage:

- They were persecuted when they came because they couldn't speak English. This was the lot of any new ethnic group that came to America.
- They were persecuted because their Christian brand was rooted in pietism rather than Anglican, Catholic, or Lutheran.
- They were persecuted because they were poor. Many came for economic benefit.

Mind you these people were the whitest of the white! They were a hard working lot and soon became part of America's great settlers of the northern parts of the country—from Brooklyn to Chicago to Minneapolis and on to Seattle.

The denomination reflected much of their heritage; local autonomy and reliance on lay (not ordained) leadership was respected. They resisted national credentialing, because in their minds, it surrendered local autonomy.

The Scandinavians kept in touch with their spiritual brothers and sisters in Scandinavia. Those back in the "old country" encouraged them to see the new life in America as a spiritual pilgrimage. When we consider this great heritage and all of the people who laid the foundation of who we are today, we realize we owe them a debt to remember.

Part of what that means is realizing that we who are now "the establishment" must welcome the "new Scandinavians"— except these new Scandinavians are not from Scandinavia. They are red and yellow, black and brown, and from places like Mexico, Congo, and the Philippines.

The ministry of Immigrant Hope is our effort to encode what we have learned. These new immigrants, like the Scandinavian immigrants who started the EFCA, do not often speak English. They are strangers to our culture and typically come with little financial resources. Nevertheless, we as a denomination should love and welcome these strangers—it is part of our heritage.

It is true that the immigration context is different today, but we ought not to think that our immigration law is such a sterling example of truth and justice. What we are saying is that God's view of the alien is our standard and his standard is simple — love the alien among you.

As you can see, when done well, the story has the potential to become viral and a point of organizational pride. You have just given the bridge builders and advocates among you a rallying cry. You will hear the cautious repeating it to the neutralists as a way to bring them along. You've even appealed to the traditionalists and honored their concerns. When combined with a biblical apologetic and systematic prayer, the multi-ethnic story tied to your founding DNA helps to create the splash of racial transcendence that will ripple through your culture.

What I am stressing is to keep the main thing the main thing. Don't compartmentalize your multi-ethnic change effort as just another new initiative, because it isn't. What you are asking people to do is grow in their faith enough to love their neighbors as themselves. It is a process of spiritual growth.

Develop an organized regular system of prayer for your organization's multi-ethnic desires. Create a biblical apologetic for multi-ethnicity. Also create a story that ties the valuable traditions of the past with the present multi-ethnic direction of the future to connect your founding DNA to the need for multi-ethnicity. Develop a plan to communicate and make this accessible for all organizational stakeholders.

NOTES

1. Robert D. Putnam and David E. Campbell, *American Grace: How Religion Divides and Unites Us* (New York: Simon & Schuster, 2010).

2. The definition is taken from my notes from a leaders' gathering at the Duke Center for Reconciliation, Durham, North Carolina, in 2008.

CHANGING
THE ETHNIC GAME

It is much better to initiate change when you can than react to it. Generally speaking, all good leaders are change agents toward vibrant, organizational culture where people can flourish and be all God made them to be. The matter of bold, transformative leadership is big in any change process. Add on the complexity of racialization, navigating ethnic borders, and messing with founding DNA, and the process becomes even bigger. Leading multi-ethnic change is rough, but very doable. Don't let the roughness of the terrain fool you into thinking that it is an impossible task.

In our base text of Acts 6:1–7, the apostles made direct, administrative changes. They were structured one way to meet the needs of the church during a particular season. When that season changed, they were more than willing to adjust. Smart leaders realize they are not slaves to structures or traditions. Structures are designed to serve the season the organization is in. Along with this, when seasons change, personnel changes are sometimes necessary. I have never seen a multiethnic change process where new structures, policies, practices, procedures, and people were not needed.

The genius of the leaders in Acts 6 was that they were able to make significant organizational changes (vv. 2–6) while keeping the organizational vision fresh and maintaining high morale (v. 7). This is what we are shooting for in the asset-based philosophy and change process. It is our main leadership responsibility.

BENEVOLENT DICTATORS

At the beginning of the book, I advocated that you not read this book alone, because the reality is that if any serious traction is going to take place, it will not be solely up to you. It will be up to God, you, and your decision-makers. I believe as a general principle that leading alone is not a great way to operate, mainly because you eliminate any possibility of practicing transformative leadership.

Some of you reading this may believe strongly in being a benevolent dictator. However, I guarantee that you will not succeed with this change process by using that style of leadership. Leading the multi-ethnic change process like a benevolent dictator is treacherous territory and a road you don't want to take.

I know our American, individualistic mind-set is to go all "Lara Croft" or "Rambo" when we want to make things happen that we are passionate about. Like those action characters, you may get what you want, but in the end you will leave a lot of destruction behind.

We need to be much more communal in our strategies. We want to lead a process where everybody emerges with their dignities intact. Leading through teams is much more beneficial and way more effective. It will change your organizational culture and make multi-ethnicity a part of the normal way of doing things.

I am a big fan of college football, particularly the Ohio State Buckeyes. Ohio State is known to have one of the best marching bands around. They are led on the field by a high-stepping, show-stopping drum major. The drum major may appear to be operating as a lone ranger, but that is not the case. He or she has worked numerous hours to stay in step with the rest of the marching band. And the drum major follows the lead of the marching band director. Think of God as the band director, major decision-makers as the drum majors, and the rest of the stakeholders as the band. I have learned the value of this metaphor the hard way. My personality and leadership style naturally leans toward being a benevolent dictator. I have paid the "dumb tax" in all of my ministry stops of trying to lead multi-ethnic change by myself. I have learned from my mistakes, and that is why I am taking the time to implore you to not go down the lonesome leadership road. Let me briefly share five of the dumb taxes I have paid.

First, I only have a limited set of tools in my skills toolbox. I can only fix the problems with the tools available, and if all I have is a hammer and the fix requires a saw, I'm stuck. This means advancing only through my own limitations and solving a narrow set of problems, leading to some change. But the change is more like addition. If addition is to become multiplication, I must find people with other tools and work with them, multiplying efforts.

Second, lonesome leadership leads to arrogance when humility is needed. I am thinking more highly of myself than I should when I think *all* the organizational answers lie with me. This type of prideful thinking leads to things being about me instead of the organization God has entrusted me to lead. Everything I do is done through healthy teams, where their strengths compensate for my weaknesses.

Third, at times I have set myself up for inevitable failure by leading alone. It unnecessarily limits my sphere of influence within the organization. Eventually, if I only depend upon myself, I will hit a glass ceiling. By effectively involving a team in the change effort, ideas immediately cause positive ripples across the organization.

Fourth, I have a bias. When examining a presenting issue, all assessments and conclusions are slanted toward my particular worldview. It is the reality of the human condition. A team with different perspectives that regularly engages in robust dialogue helps bring full consciousness to what needs to be done.

Fifth, I have found that benevolent dictators eventually have no followers. Leading alone is lonely. The end of the road is often being put in an organizational silo and feeling personally isolated. Even if you could be successful leading alone, God made the Christian life to be lived in community, not isolation, and we need to acknowledge this as we lead the change process.

If you are reading this alone, stop and bring decision-makers into the loop—now! I am trying to save you a lot of wasted energy and heartache of trying to be the lone change agent. Your decision-makers have to be on board with both the philosophy and process if any lasting change is going to happen. Bringing them on board is your starting point.

THE CRITERIA FOR CHANGE

Now that you understand that you need a team of implementation leaders around you, let's talk about the team itself.

Recruit Transformative People

My first principle for multi-ethnic change is to get the right people around you. More times than not, it is the people at the top of the organizational chart who are the cause of building a culture of either tweaking or transformation. Tweaking is fear-based change as opposed to Word-based and Spirit-filled. You cannot embark on this journey from the posture of being afraid to rock the boat. You might as well face the reality that implementing multi-ethnic change is a boat rocker. This is not a cruise ship outing; it's white-water rafting, and you will not be able to tweak your way to success.

We talked in chapter 4 about the camps people are in (bridge builders, advocates, cautious, neutralists, traditionalists). You can see how these camps might hurt or help sustain performance. When it comes to multi-ethnicity, if you have bridge builders and advocates in a majority of your decision-maker positions, things will take off. If you have a bunch of people from the cautious camp, you will probably go in the right direction but at an incremental, slow pace. If neutralists and traditionalists dominate, good luck! They cannot take the organization where it needs to go from a multi-ethnic perspective. When they were hired, they probably were not vetted for multi-ethnic awareness and experience. They may not even have the skill set to move forward. Organizational charts matter. If people at the top don't get it, the rest of the organization will not progress. It's like speaking Latin (a dead language) to people who only know English.

Rare is the situation where gutsy decisions do not have to be made about C-, board-, staff-, or director-level leadership when getting serious about the multi-ethnic change process. At times this could be a tricky situation. You might have someone who is great at doing certain tasks but clueless on the multi-ethnic front. Because of this, a bottle-neck develops around the person, holding up things. This is because implementing multi-ethnicity is a process of recalibrating the organization for meeting the organizational mission.

When we hire, we are pros at screening for reputation and whether someone is wise in the field for which we are hiring. The multi-ethnic criteria fits under the broader umbrella of being Spirit-filled, and that is much harder to screen for. Leadership is spiritual in our organizations, and if someone is not showing the ability to love a neighbor, it is a sin. Nobody would blink if someone was let go for a sexual moral failure, but try selling the idea of letting someone go for "benign" racism, and it will probably won't go over well.

I hope that you don't think I am being a control freak. I firmly believe in honoring people for their faithful service, even if they don't quite understand multi-ethnicity. But I also believe Christian leadership is a sacred trust of God's mission, and I know that to understand the significance of loving our neighbors as ourselves requires us to be daring. After all, Jesus made it the second greatest commandment and likened it to the first (Matt. 22:37–40). When you sense changes have to be made, I encourage you to be gracious but to not back down from making them. Each day of apathy, color blindness, and confusion leads to the existence of an organization beautifully equipped to serve an ethnic world of the past.

Charge the Multi-Ethnic Hill

The second principle is being willing to die on the multi-ethnic hill. If you are not willing to get fired or resign over implementing multi-ethnic changes, then don't even start the process. When approached about being the main leader to initiate multi-ethnic change for the EFCA, I told the president I would take on the challenge for three years. When he asked why only three, I said, "Because neither of us knows if the EFCA organizational culture can handle the changes I am going to advocate for." I told him it will take me at least that long to figure out if the decision-makers are serious. I am a skeptic at heart and see better than I hear. I told myself, at the three-year point, I will either make a decision to resign, because I think the organization is not serious, or I will be all in. I am happy to report I am going on year six, and things are going well.

As I write this, one organization I am consulting with is making budget cuts. Their CFO doesn't understand the goal of becoming more multi-ethnic. When it is time to make cuts, he always aggressively recommends gutting the diversity programs. During one of the decision-making meetings, one of the senior vice presidents said point blank to the president, "If we gut the diversity program, I will resign," and he meant it to the core of his being. We all have hills we die on. You have to decide if you are willing to die on this one.

If you don't make it a hill to die on, you will end up doing more harm than good by employing "push hard, then pull back" tactics.

The ethnics who value diversity, bridge builders, and advocates will feel betrayed; the cautious, neutralists, and traditionalists will sniff out that you are not truly committed, and they'll continue to do the same old thing. It is the quickest way to kill organizational morale.

Seek Outside Input

The third principle for multi-ethnic change is to include outside voices. I mentioned this in chapter 4. On the surface, it looks like a contradiction to the inside-out part of the asset-based philosophy, but it's not. I recommend you bring in outside voices is to make sure that your internal focus does not become a toxic environment.

And like in nature, when things become internally toxic, it has the potential to be a killer. This is especially true if this whole multi-ethnic concept is relatively new to your organization. You need something to kick-start new ideas and ways of thinking. If you don't bring someone from the outside in, it will leave you vulnerable to groupthink, an actual phenomenon that happens within organizations. Generally speaking, it is when normal organizational opinion is pursued and direction taken even when there is no evidence that it will be productive. There may be clear evidence of other options that will solve the presenting issues, but people just won't go there. A skilled outside voice that points out the elephants in the room, names the critical issues, and suggests solutions is just what the doctor ordered for the needs of the organizational soul.

However, the advisors can't be any outside voices. They have to be people who have your best interests in mind. They have to operate with tremendous amounts of grace and humility and be bold enough to challenge old perspectives. The issues they may stir up will probably be unpopular, but it is necessary for someone to point them out, because if not done, the long-term sustainability of your change process is at stake.

GENERAL GAME CHANGERS

In the United States, the health of our faith is dependent on our ability to learn how to demographically coexist together. If we don't figure it out, we are putting the effective demonstration of the gospel in peril. Gone are the days where it is acceptable to be 100 percent white in a community with 60 percent people of color. To unbelievers who live in an integrated society, that looks like an impotent gospel.

The term *transformational leadership* is one I've alluded to throughout this book. Let me take time here to be more specific about what I mean. A simple way I define it is getting people to do what they won't naturally do. It is the game changer in the multi-ethnic change process. This type of leadership designs change in a way that brings optimistic energy. It is practicing thoughtful formation of Word-based, Spirit-filled, innovative strategies. I've been encouraging you to put the right leaders in place. Their primary task is to bring transformation to the policies, practices, and procedures of your organization that will cause ethnic others to self-select to become a part of your mission. It is organizational rejuvenation at its finest.

Transformational leadership will be the glue that makes the value of multi-ethnicity advocated in Scripture stick across the organization. It is the ripples of the ripple effect. Personally, we are to practice what we preach; and corporately, we are to preach what we practice. This is the heart of building the multi-ethnic kingdom.

Because of racialization and ethnic borders, there will be constant, mainly subconscious, pushback. This is natural, because organizations have the tendency to choose the path of least resistance. Being transformational interrupts the slide toward comfort. It is to be myopically focused and always craving more effectiveness.

Every multi-ethnic, organizational transformation will have a unique story. With this in mind, let me suggest several transformational components that successful organizations possess for leading toward God's multi-ethnic kingdom. The name of the meal prepared may change so to speak, but they will all have these ingredients.

Major Decision-Makers Are Front and Center

This is the practical application of a top-down philosophy. Probably the best way to symbolize just how important this is to the organization is for senior leaders to constantly advocate for the change. Noticeable, vigilant communication from this group exponentially increases the chances of eliminating the dandelion effect.

Not only do they create and maintain the innovation stage, but they also actively work against the inertia stage. They spearhead successful change by providing backup and pushing for goals to be met. There is a clear communication plan to make sure that there are no mixed messages sent throughout the organization. Every multi-ethnic change process needs champions for the cause.

The larger the organization you lead, the more likely you already have effective multi-ethnic change going on that you don't have a clue about. I am amazed that although I have been on the job for six years, I am constantly unearthing EFCA churches that are effectively doing multi-ethnic ministry that I did not know about. When they find out about what I do and learn they aren't alone, it is always a powerful moment. It means a lot to them that their passion is represented at the senior level of leadership and that they are part of an intentional denomination-wide effort. It strengthens their will to keep pursuing God's call on their lives and makes them even more loyal to the EFCA. It galvanizes support and increases the potential for building critical mass.

There is no such thing as senior leadership advocating multiethnicity too much. Every audience, whether large or small, needs to know just how committed to multi-ethnicity you are. It will be the biggest factor in convincing the cautious, neutralists, and even some traditionalists to get on board and embrace the change.

In terms of up-front decision-makers, let's go back to Acts 6. Besides having a good reputation, being wise, and being Spirit-filled, there was also another specific qualification that, although not overtly spelled out, was huge. In verse 5, do you notice something about the names of those put in leadership? They are all of Greek origin.

This suggests two things. First, they definitely were not ignoring ethnicity in the leadership selection process. And second, the leadership selected were probably part of the offended Grecian Jew church membership. Please don't overlook this fact based on modern-day politics. Nowadays people call this "affirmative action." I'm not here to be political but biblical. I don't think this means that ethnic people should automatically be in charge of the change effort or that quotas should be implemented (revisit chapter 3). After all, being Greek was only one of the requirements. It was the other three characteristics that made being Greek the game changer. Following the principles laid out in Acts 6, you need people of color up front who get it.

What is "it"? It is racialization, ethnic border negotiation, your founding DNA, loving neighbors, dependency on God, and effectively negotiating organizational polity. Finding these individuals who are ethnic and willing to serve is akin to hitting a grand slam. But if you put people who are rented or zealous in lead roles and who do not get it, you can prepare for the worst. Their ethnicity won't save them from leadership disaster.

There Is Either a Formal or Informal All-In, Zero-Tolerance Policy

At both Cincinnati Christian and the EFCA, I started off as a one-man department given the responsibility of rippling the multi-ethnic efforts across the entire organization. In my benevolent dictator slant, I actually negotiated this type of setup in the job description. It's not the wisest way to approach things.

Experience has taught me that not involving everyone leaves the impression that organizational diversity initiatives are optional. My leadership personality smacked right up against the wall of reality. A shift had to be made in order for me to be more effective. Instead of me being the major initiator, I now spend most of my time coaching the coaches, so to speak.

My EFCA responsibilities now reflect how much diversity of all kinds is an organizational priority. We expect it to be a part of everyone's job responsibilities in some form or another. I work side by side with our president, CFO, senior development officer, and national and international vice presidents to develop strategic action plans. The hope is to integrate all staff into the process.

Of course the expectation regarding the level of commitment looks different for an accountant than it does for a missionary or pastor. But the embracing of what we call our "all people" value is a denomination-wide expectation. Our desire is to touch all of our organizational members.

They Are Not the French Army

In military circles, the French army is known more for their ability to tactically retreat than for impressive victories. Here is a given: You will spend a lot of effort planning and leading diversity efforts, and you will have some failures. Accept mistakes as part of the learning process instead of a signal to retreat to the ethnic status quo.

Leadership fatigue is a real threat. I've run across many people who have completed the dandelion process and decide to give it up. Keep tackling the hard-hitting presenting issues, since many times the first run will not be successful. But it sets you up well for the second or even third run. Examining failed past efforts and mistakes is important and tremendously helpful. Knowing what *not* to do is just as valuable as knowing what to do.

Of course, at some point, you might have to prayerfully make a decision. First, second, and third runs are to be expected. Forty-eighth, forty-ninth, and fiftieth runs are not. It may be that you find yourself in a position that it's time to "shake the dust off your feet" and move on (Matt. 10:14). Don't feel guilty if this is the case or if you feel like you have wasted your efforts. If one church, college, or nonprofit won't listen, trust God and find an organization that will and apply the lessons you learned in your new leadership call.

They Measure Success as a Value, Not Simply as Numbers

Numbers won't tell the whole story. When I pastored at River of Life, sometimes I had talks with young men who were lured to enter the financially lucrative trade of drug dealing. "Pastor, why would I give up this money to go work for minimum wage?" was always a question. My typical response was, "Well, if it's about the money, don't. But if it's about living a purposeful life and following Jesus, you must. You have a life-changing decision to make." The ones for whom it was only about the number of dollar bills unfortunately always ended up either dead or in jail, and the ones for whom following Christ was a value, we worked to transition them into legitimate vocations.

Remember that we are framing multi-ethnicity as spiritual growth. If you move away from this, you may be tempted to implement measures that will build numbers but not cause people to become like Christ. I know of some organizations that simply buy integration with salaries and benefits packages. They may be multicolored, but they are far from multi-ethnic. And their people are not transformed.

I've stressed throughout this book that we reach success when we institute multi-ethnic change as a kingdom value. That is more times than not a reachable goal. Maybe not as fast as you would like, but you can get there. The problem with focusing on numbers is that if you draw the numbers without building the kingdom value, you have missed the whole biblical point. If it is only about the numbers, it is fool's gold. Numbers are not everything. In fact, when it comes to multi-ethnicity, it may be the worst way to measure things. You may be in a particular geographic location that makes gathering numbers extremely difficult. Or your organization may have 95 percent neutralists and traditionalists within decision-making positions. In neither instance will you see numbers anytime soon. Focus on the value, and the numbers will come.

A better measure of success is the percentage of people who are getting it. That is one thing to definitely measure, probably as a soft metric. What are you doing to ensure that as many people as possible are getting it? If you are located in a geographical place that lends itself to ethnic diversity, the more people on your staff who get it, the greater your numerical success will be.

They Broaden the Diversity Agenda

Part of being in a post-civil rights era is to avoid isolating race as the only part of personal identity relating to multi-ethnicity. This attitude will come to light when you implement a multi-ethnic change process. It is nearly impossible to separate race from social class and gender. People are going to want to know what the plan is for other forms of diversity. Broadening the agenda could lessen the emphasis on ethnic diversity. However, we are not dealing with reality if we ignore the calls for diversity in gender, social class, and even clarification of how to address the homosexual-identified lifestyle. I believe that it is just part of the territory for the twenty-first century.

My primary response is to frame the whole issue as "in and out" group dynamics. The "other" is the other, whether they are the other racial group, the other social class or sexuality group, or the other in the forms of age or disability. I have a training team whose primary function is to develop specific training for topics such as poverty, gender, and sexuality.

The one thing that binds all the elements of changing the ethnic game together is the level of determination of the leadership. Decision-makers should expect major pockets of resistance. There will be a variety of motivations for the resistance, but rest assured, it will be there. People naturally gravitate toward keeping the status quo.

Whether or not your organization moves forward will often simply come down to how determined and unified the leadership is. Determination involves setting the course and not wavering. It means painting a picture of a preferred future, communicating it repeatedly, and holding people accountable. When this is done, change happens.

PUTTING IT
ALL TOGETHER

Here is my best-case scenario. You and other decision-makers have read this book and are on board with understanding racialization, ethnic borders, and unintentonality. Everyone believes in the asset-based philosophy of inside out, top down, and all in. You all agree that multi-ethnic change is a call to spiritual growth, have kick-started the innovation stage, and are being as transformative as leaders can be. There is one final thing left to do in this process, and that is to strategically plan for multi-ethnic change. This is the best way to align people and hold them accountable.

Actually, the steps are not as neat and sequential as you just read. In reality you will be working on multiple things at the same time and focusing on some phases more than others depending on circumstances. As work is being done, it is extremely helpful to keep all your efforts organized and in sync with one another. That's why you need a strategic plan.

The first step is to form an implementation team. In Acts 6, the standards used to select leaders were good reputation, wisdom, and being filled with the Spirit (vv. 2–4). Other characteristics of good team members are that they are in sync with organizational theology and philosophy of ministry, are strategic thinkers, and are good relationally. I would recommend that the leader of the team be a senior leadership-level individual who is a bridge builder or advocate.

The implementation team has two primary tasks. The first is planning organizational alignment, which is constructively positioning people and tasks. The second is providing organizational accountability, which is holding people responsible for an accounting of their activities. Without intentional alignment and accountability, efforts can quickly get sidetracked, misunderstandings can happen, and the door is left wide open for the inertia cycle to start. It also can lead to people doing their own thing in their own way. There is no I in team but there is an M and E!

Alignment and accountability are not measured by whether team members have a good relationship with one another or by spiritual "feel goods" like emotionally encouraging prayer times. They are also not measured by everybody giving good reports on how things are going. These are great team dynamics but not the goal the team should be shooting for. Both alignment and accountability are about successfully accomplishing the mission. Both are tools to help the team point the organization in the right direction and galvanize capacities and gifts to create progress.

Great team dynamics can actually hurt the process. If we are not careful, teams can get together and leave the room feeling good without actually accomplishing anything. Most likely this type of scenario is because team identity has been formed around the wrong things. Team identity needs to primarily be formed around workflow.

FRAMING THE MULTI-ETHNIC PICTURE

Strategic planning is the primary purpose of your implementation team. I believe the best way to operate is to develop a rhythm: make a plan, do the plan, check the plan, and adjust to improve the plan.[1] For every major task to be accomplished, I recommend this cycle. However, before you begin planning, there is a major step of clarity that must be taken.

My colleague T. J. Addington uses the illustration of a sandbox to help bring organizational clarity as a whole.[2] He says that there are four areas every on which organization needs to focus in order to maintain its vision (mission, guiding principles, central ministry focus, and culture). I maintain that, in regard to multi-ethnicity, there are four areas of focus to keep your organization in the innovation stage. Playing off of Addington's sandbox, I call it "developing a multi-ethnic picture frame." The multi-ethnic picture frame is the highest form of clarity for your team. It will give teammates a unifying philosophy on how to operate.

The priority is to keep efforts squarely in the innovation stage and out of the inertia stage. Leaders should acknowledge the complexity of the task of ethnic diversity from the staff's point of view. Staff will be watching closely to see if senior leadership is serious about bringing change, and sometimes complaining that diversity is being forced upon them. A common response is, "I have my regular job, and then I have this diversity stuff. I don't know how the two work together," or, "I wasn't hired to do this."

Work avoidance is a common response, but the motive doesn't matter because the outcome is the same: inertia. The multi-ethnic change process is not something to leave up to chance. Clear expectations must be put in place and accounted for. To invoke alignment and accountability and to usher in clarity to the people you lead, there are four basic questions that need to be addressed by the team:

- How does multi-ethnicity tie in to the organizational mission?
- What core commitments need to be made for multi-ethnicity to prosper?

- What will the organization laser focus on to become more multi-ethnic?

- What type of environment needs to exist for the value of multi-ethnicity to thrive?

Think of these as the four sides of your multi-ethnic picture frame: mission, core commitments, laser focus, and environment. The following is what the EFCA developed:

MISSION

EFCA exists to glorify God by
multiplying healthy churches among all people.

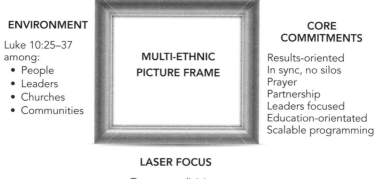

ENVIRONMENT

Luke 10:25–37
among:
- People
- Leaders
- Churches
- Communities

MULTI-ETHNIC
PICTURE FRAME

CORE
COMMITMENTS

Results-oriented
In sync, no silos
Prayer
Partnership
Leaders focused
Education-orientated
Scalable programming

LASER FOCUS

To reverse division,
multiplying kingdom growth

Once all these sides have been made clear, the challenge for the team is to align everyone and hold them accountable, so that everyone is working on painting the same multi-ethnic picture. Once the picture is painted, clear roles for specific people can be developed through accountability action plans.

Mission Integration

As I've said multiple times, always remember to connect founding DNA. Multi-ethnicity cannot be left twisting in the wind as a side project. Priorities must be established, and it must be clearly communicated why ethnic diversity as a value is critical to the mission.

The compass of the plan is always 100 percent of the time the mission of the organization. It is essential that organizational diversity efforts are viewed as crucial to the fulfillment of your organization's mission. Otherwise, the multi-ethnic change process will sit in isolation, be marginalized, and sink to low-priority status. A mission statement created with an overt declaration toward multi-ethnicity would be ideal. The EFCA mission statement is: "To glorify God by multiplying healthy churches among all people." The phrase "all people" stands out strongly as a value. In fact, it was the creation of this statement in the 1990s that eventually led to me being hired in 2007.

Once the "all people" part of the statement was inserted, a biblical diversity task force was created by a directive from the president and board of directors to hold the denomination accountable. The task force was committed to three main initiatives:

• Develop and articulate a biblical apologetic for diversity and reconciliation.

- Conduct a review of the EFCA national office and its systems, and address institutional aspects of racism and homogeneity (such as personnel policies and hiring).
- Create deliverable tools to equip EFCA churches in living out biblical principles of unity across racial lines.

My job was created to move this task force's dreams forward. And it all started with putting two little words in the mission statement.

However, I understand that mission statements in some places are sacred cows, never to be altered. If you can't change it, work with it. The key is to tie it somehow to your diversity efforts. Whatever is done for the sake of diversity will die out if leaders can't answer how it makes the organization meet its stated reason for existence.

Core Commitments

Core commitments are the equivalent to giving people the rules and strategy of the game. I remember when I was ten years old, meeting some kids who were playing soccer in a park. They asked me if I wanted to play. I said sure and joined in the game. There was just one problem: I had no idea how to play. I just ran wherever the ball went and tried to kick it. If you know soccer, you know that is not how it is played. I might have the potential to be the best soccer player ever, but if I don't know the rules, nobody will ever know how good I could be. In your multi-ethnic efforts, people need guiding principles that the organization is committed to following. These commitments define the rules of operation and should be measurable. They are the behavioral guidelines.

The measurable part is critical, because it can help you hold people accountable. If utilized properly, the core commitments can be a tremendous source of clarity. First, they define for all involved the fundamental beliefs to which you want everyone to adhere. Second, when you put them all together, they create the environment for innovation to occur, setting the stage for organizational change. When everybody understands what is expected, the organization can now move toward alignment of talent and resources. Lastly, everyone knows where fixed boundaries are. This goes a long way toward preventing misunderstandings. Core commitments are a tremendous empowerment tool because they help people figure out what are good ideas as opposed to great ideas. They also help people decide where they should spend their time and energy, and they chart your unique course of how ethnic diversity will develop.

Here are my team's guiding principles. The first letter of each core commitment forms the acronym RIPPLES. This is the grid through which we run all ideas. If the idea is consistent with these seven items, then it is viable for us to do:

- Results-oriented
- In sync, no silos

- Prayer

- Partnership

- Leaders focused

- Education-oriented

- Scalable programming

Laser Focus

By laser focus I mean figuring out what is the primary thing that must be done every day for your organization to progress multi-ethnically. It is the serious action that will bring the maximum results. Taking into consideration your mission, it is the one thing that you must focus on with a laser-like intensity. Figuring this out is a big piece of the puzzle. It will point you in the direction of how to best utilize the resources and people you have available. It will focus the team on maximizing the ministry opportunities it has before it.

Generally speaking, for Christian leadership, the laser focus is Ephesians 4:12–13: "To prepare God's people for works of service, so that the body of Christ may be built up, until we all reach unity in the faith and in the knowledge of the Son of God and become mature, attaining to the whole measure of the fullness of Christ." We all must play off of that in some way.

For my team, our laser focus is to help EFCA leaders reverse societal division in order to multiply kingdom growth. Our hope is that by training our pastors and district leaders in this they will lead churches that focus on balancing proclamation and demonstration of the gospel.

Environment

When it comes to multi-ethnicity, organizational environment is huge. You can have all the other sides of the frame built, but if this one does not come together, it doesn't matter what you do in the others. An environment must be created for the ethnic other to prosper.

In theory, our Christian organizational environments should readily welcome ethnic inclusion. However, as I have pointed out earlier on numerous occasions, this is not the case most of the time. I have a statement I use a lot when training: "The ethnic other is too often welcome but not invited." Have you ever been in such a situation?

I have been a "tag along" before, and many of you may relate to the awkwardness. One day I dropped by a cousin's house while he was walking out the door to go to a dinner party. At his invitation, instead of going home, I decided to accompany him. Besides my cousin, I didn't know anyone, their inside jokes, or the reason for the party. Everyone was cordial, but it was pretty clear I didn't belong.

That is what environment is about—creating a space of belonging for people who are ethnically different. I can't tell you how many leaders have told me that other ethnic groups are welcome but they never show up. I always reply, "Have you asked yourself why?" If they are not showing up (assuming there are plenty who could), that is the question.

I've thrown around the words *policies*, *practices*, and *procedures* a lot in this book. Let me unpack these a bit because these three things control your environment. A policy is a definite course of action adopted for the sake of expediency; a practice is a habit or custom that is considered normal; and a procedure refers to processes. I'll take something as simple as a worship service. It may be the most vivid and familiar example of Christian ethnic captivity.

How long should the service last? In some churches, the policy is one hour. In others the policy is four hours. The time policy has every-thing to do with ethnic values. What is the normal type of music? Depending on Christian tradition and ethnicity, it will be either high or low energy, consist of long or short musical sets, and be emotionally expressive or toned down. The practices are totally rooted in ethnic boundaries. What about when it is time for the sermon? How should the service proceed? Should the sermon have many Scripture refer-ences or just one passage? Should it be full of narrative stories or hard, rational facts? Should it be aimed at the most spiritually mature in the audience and treated like a lecture or have a few inspirational, relevant points and end with a time of celebrative exhortations? Like policies and practices, the procedure is all in ethnic values.

The key is to build a hybrid ethnic environment. True multi-ethnic organizations are where policies, practices, and procedures take into account a multitude of ethnic perspectives. I remember talking to a member of the EFCA ordination committee one day and comparing notes on how we became ordained.

He was ordained in a white church and denomination, where basically the policy, practice, and procedure resembled a college course. I was ordained in a traditional African-American church where I didn't write one paper. It was based on an apprenticeship model of shadowing the pastor, doing assigned tasks, and proving my call through the observation of my character. Which one is right? Both seem to have worked fine for us, since we both have been in fruitful ministries for close to two decades. A present challenge for us at the EFCA is how to build such a hybrid ordination process.

Another big part of environment is the handling of racial incidents. Do we shy away and ignore them, or do we actively work to understand the differences, act on the commonalities, and find common ground? That was the way of the early church. Ethnic stakeholders will tolerate slights if they know that the leadership wants them there and is proactive in solving problems.

My team has a hope of creating environments like that of Luke 10:25–37 among our people, leaders, churches, and communities. We desire for our constituents to love their neighbors as themselves through the demonstration of the gospel. We want to create a radical atmosphere that causes people to love one another across all boundaries for the sake of Christ.

CONCLUSION

I've mentioned before that leading multi-ethnic change is more art than science and is highly contingent and situational. It's like a chameleon, changing colors based on the situation it finds itself in, but at the end of the day it is still a chameleon. Although you have read my story, I want to be very clear—there is no one-size-fits-all formula for success. But we can share principles of what we have learned in the hopes that they will help others, contributing to the pool of wisdom available on the topic. So here is a brief summary of the principles I have outlined.

1. Ethnic diversity was a kingdom priority for Jesus and the early church; therefore it should be one for every Christian organization.

2. The Bible depicts the nations as being in a family feud, and it is our job to model a family reunion.

3. Ethnicity plays a huge role in influencing our personal identities, creating ethnic borders. Personal identity is based on individual choices and the society we live in. These two things are attached at the hip and never are independent of each other.

4. Racialization is the process in which people impose a racial element into a social situation, often to oppress people. It is prevalent within the United States and is why color blindness is not the answer.

5. Every Christian organization possesses founding DNA, and this DNA either hurts or hinders multi-ethnic efforts.

6. We must intentionally guard against the dandelion effect, a pattern of Christian organizations making an energetic run at ethnic diversity only to see inertia kick in after a few years.

7. Multi-ethnicity within our organizations should be framed as spiritual growth to guard against the societal attitude of racial tolerance. Otherwise racial tolerance will fill the void for motivation, which in the long run will not serve our interests.

8. Lasting change comes from having the right people in the right spots and practicing transformative, team leadership.

9. In order to keep the vision at the forefront and stay in the innovation cycle, we must systematically focus on and hold ourselves accountable to four areas: mission, core commitments, laser focus, and environment.

10. Implement a rhythm of plan, do, check, and adjust.

I began this book by pointing out that I do not consider myself a guru. I am just adding to an ever-growing number of voices that are trying to help people think through multi-ethnic leadership. My assessment of the leadership landscape is that all of us who are attempting multi-ethnic change are works in progress. We are actively trying to figure out how to make this all work in a way that is beneficial to the body of Christ. The one thing we know for sure is that ethnic diversity is here to stay and more and more leaders than ever before will be signing up for duty. So I will end this book by issuing an invitation.

I desire to be a part of a network of learners who are preparing their organizations for a majority-minority, multi-ethnic America. We need to build knowledge together. I would love to hear from you. Share with me (alvin.sanders87@gmail.com) your multi-ethnic picture frames, and I would love to see the strategic plans you develop. Interact with me on my blog (www.alvin.sanders.net). Follow me on Twitter (AlvinSanders1), and I'll follow back. Let's continue the conversation!

May the Lord bless your efforts.

NOTES

1. The rhythm of plan, do, check, and adjust is a form of LEAN thinking. It is very common in the business world and many organizations are adapting it for nonprofits. To learn more, see Robert O. Martichenko, *Everything I Know about LEAN I Learned in First Grade* (Cambridge, Mass.: Lean Enterprise Institute, 2008).

2. T. J. Addington, *Leading from the Sandbox: How to Develop, Empower, and Release High-Impact Ministry Teams* (Colorado Springs: NavPress, 2010).

LEARNING LAB

In the introduction of this book, I highly encouraged you to read this book within a Christian leadership community. In an effort to help the group digest the material, use this chapter-by-chapter discussion guide. By doing so, you will create a dynamic leadership learning time that will go a long way in helping you engage multi-ethnicity within your organization.

INTRODUCTION

Summary

A common myth is that you can take a secular diversity program, "Christianize" it, and be good to go. This is not sufficient because we as Christian leaders have a unique role in this world. We are charged to lead the citizens of the kingdom of God. Multi-ethnicity is a kingdom priority measured by the sincere work we do to achieve it.

The philosophy that undergirds secular diversity efforts is not designed for Christian organizations. The main reason they won't work is that organizational cultures are too different. By *organizational culture*, I'm referring to the pattern of development that is reflected in our policies (courses of action), practices (habits and customs), and procedures (day-to-day rituals). The combination of being both Christian and nonprofit means that our organizational cultures typically have dynamics to be accounted for that others don't.

There are three general challenges we all face. The first is rooted in ethnic borders. Ethnic borders are those cultural traits we tightly hold on to that define our ethnic identities. Most ethnic folk are aware of theirs while most whites are not. Most people, regardless of ethnicity, are typically not very flexible in moving the borders. Unearthing and negotiating these is half the battle.

The second challenge is racialization. According to authors Michael Emerson and Christian Smith, "A racialized society is a society wherein race matters profoundly for differences in life experiences, life opportunities, and social relationships. . . . [It is one] that allocates different economic, political, social, and even psychological rewards to groups along racial lines."[1] Racialization is why color blindness is not the answer and actually a big contributor to establishing ethnic borders.

The third challenge is unintentionality. Most Christian organizations did not have multi-ethnic in mind when they started, and the Christian traditions from which our institutions sprung are not all the same. We all possess what I call founding DNA. Our diversity efforts must be connected with this.

In many ways, leading a multi-ethnic transition may be unlike anything you have attempted to lead before. The leadership required is highly situational and contingent. It is more of an art than a science. I capture the type of leadership needed by using the term *asset-based diversity development*. This guides leaders to leverage change by unlocking the organization's capacities and gifts rather than leading from a base of deficiencies and needs caused by the three challenges above.

This leadership philosophy serves as your diversity bridge and requires making basic shifts in thinking. The philosophy is inside out, top down, and all in. The process is Word-based, Spirit-filled, team and transformative in nature, and implements accountable alignment.

The first shift to be made is from secular to spiritual. Theories of secular diversity are helpful and informative but should never serve as the foundation for Christian integration efforts. Multi-ethnicity efforts based on secularized notions of diversity often lead to little spiritual impact because their foundation is not based in Scripture. Our number one asset is the Bible.

The second shift is from tweaking to transformative leadership. Getting to multi-ethnicity is not something where you can tweak a few things and move on. Tweaking is fear-based change. We are afraid to significantly rock the boat, so we hope we can tweak our way out of our predicaments. It never works.

The last shift is from accidental to accountability and alignment. What else is needed to turn your good intentions into good fruit? Your followers need boundaries because boundaries give clarity. If your strategy is fuzzy to you, it will be a fog to the people you lead. People need to be pointed in the right direction and then held accountable. To do so will require leadership providing a basic framework to operate in.

Discussion Questions

1. Do you believe bridging the diversity gap is a problem that can be solved? More importantly, how firmly do you believe it is a problem *worth* solving?

2. Many people feel uncomfortable when the topic of pursuing multi-ethnicity comes up, especially if their organization has never intentionally gone down this road. Other than the three challenges mentioned, why do you think this is the case?

3. Besides it being a kingdom priority, what are your top three reasons for pursuing multi-ethnicity from an organizational perspective? What are your top three reasons to *not* pursue it? How do you plan on reconciling these in order to move forward?

4. Does how you spend your time, talent, and treasure show that you have a passion for loving your ethnic neighbor? Provide life evidence to support your answer positively or negatively.

5. What do you suggest is the most important thing your organization must do to make the transition process a success?

After reading the introduction and going through the discussion questions, what are some topics you and the team should be praying about—personally and organizationally? Share and pray right now.

CHAPTER I: ETHNIC BORDERS

Summary

The Bible depicts a world of smaller, competing families, known as nations. The links that form these families—whose members share familiar origins and basics of culture, such as language, values, attitudes, and beliefs—we label as ethnic.

Ethnic borders are cultural traits we hold on to in order to define our ethnic identity. Biblically, we are never asked to give up ethnicity for some generic notion of nonethnic Christianity. Jesus embraced his ethnicity. His goal was not to eliminate ethnicity but to transcend it. The stress of the New Testament is toward a community of people making their presence known by living differently as the people of God in their geographic region. As they do this, the people of their region will know where to look for God.

Organizations that accept ethnicity as a normal part of the human experience will acknowledge, appreciate, and leverage differences instead of denigrating or ignoring them. When speaking of ethnic identity, I'm using the concept in the sense that it is the way we present who we are to others as well as ourselves. We have to recognize when constructing a sense of identity we are always partly unique and partly a creation of our society.

The mistake commonly made is to focus intensely only on our biblical selves. We possess biblical, societal, and unique selves that are constantly informing one another. They are not fixed, but flexible and always evolving. Through this constant interaction, we form our personal identities.

Many white people have never found it necessary to think deeply about what it means to be white in America, but most people of color have dealt with their ethnicities by necessity. To understand this, Andrew Walls uses the "twin forces of Christian history" to describe an indigenizing principle and a pilgrim principle.[2]

The indigenizing principle says there is no such thing as a Christian who is not heavily influenced by the society to which he or she belongs. Applying this principle to our three selves means that we must reconcile the gospel with our societal selves in order to accept Christ in our unique selves, which creates our biblical selves.

Because we are somewhat prisoners to society, we need to be liberated from many aspects of it. This liberating force is the pilgrim principle, which requires us to change some societal ethnic values to which we are bound in order to match up with biblical teachings.

The goal is to move from an ethnocentric perspective to a Christ-centered one. Based on our personal identities, we all come to the table with ethnic values. When we talk about ethnic values, we are talking about whether we consider something right or wrong based on our ethnic heritage. These values help us determine what we consider to be normal. We all have these rules of behavior—often learned innately rather than taught—and if someone violates those rules, they are considered abnormal at best and a threat at worst. These values are what make up our ethnic borders.

Our personal identities are loaded with preconceived notions based in our societal and unique selves. We want our borders to be flexible. Border flexibility consists of learning how ethnicity shapes both us and our views of others. True understanding comes from combining our heads (information) with our hearts (emotions) and with our hands (experience).

In order to expand your borders, you need to take many personal journeys of understanding in order to produce lifestyle change. The vehicle for journeys of understanding is authentic friendship and community. What I mean is having long-term, true, organic friendships where you can experience sincere community with others who are not ethnically the same. It's by far the most effective way to learn about and become more comfortable with differences.

When you regularly interact with people ethnically different through authentic relationship, it changes your values, attitudes, and beliefs about life. Being a part of a sincere community of people ethnically different from you makes you fully conscious of the world you live in.

Besides long-term authentic relationship, the next best thing toward expanding borders is authentic conversations. The more of these conversations you have, the more you learn about yourself and others.

Bridge builders recognize that differences exist, but they learn successful approaches for resolving conflict. They make border expansion part of their DNA by obtaining knowledge and applying it to their everyday living. They also provide spaces for significant communication to occur to keep misunderstandings based on ethnicity to a minimum.

We need to embrace the principle that ethnicity shapes our lives. We then need to make the adaptations necessary to further the kingdom. This is the most practical step that a ministry needs to take in order to practice reconciliation.

Discussion Questions

1. Does the notion of ethnic borders resonate with you? Explain why or why not.

2. How easy or hard is it for you to accept that part of your value system comes directly from your ethnic identity?

3. Of the ideas presented, which caught your attention? Why?

4. On a scale of one to ten with one being "not much" and ten being "very much," assign a number that reflects how strongly you identify with your ethnicity. Discuss how you determined the number.

5. What issues do you need to personally engage as a result of reading this chapter? What issues does your organization need to consider?

After reading this chapter and going through the discussion questions, what are some topics you and the team should be praying about—personally and organizationally? Share and pray right now.

CHAPTER 2: RACIALIZATION

Summary

I use the terms *race* and *ethnicity* interchangeably, even though race is technically categorizing people genetically, and ethnicity is categorizing people by shared history, cultural roots, and a sense of shared identity. I do so because most people view race and ethnicity as the same thing, even though categorizing people by biological race has been scientifically disproven.

We must accept the fact of race being an influencer of American life. Racial discrimination became a way of life within our foundational institutions. American historical record suggests that we should start with the premise that race influences everything we do in society, including leading Christian organizations. Sociologists call this phenomenon "racialization."

A racialized society is a society wherein race profoundly matters for differences in life experiences, life opportunities, and social relationships. It is one that allocates different economic, political, social, and psychological rewards to groups along racial lines. Basically, it is the process in which people impose a racial element into a social situation, often to oppress people.

As leaders we must morally manage and define what ethnicity means within our personal lives and the organizations we lead. It is impossible to overestimate the importance of this basic realization. Possessing a different moral compass from society is what is supposed to set us apart as Christians.

Because we live in a racialized society, dismissing ethnic identity through color blindness is akin to taking an immoral action. For centuries race has been a cause for a tremendous amount of human conflict. Some have no idea how their racial background naturally forms a basis for historical distrust. And it is almost unavoidable to at least partly misjudge the actions of people based on falsely learned racial expectations. Therefore, to successfully lead people to manage the meaning of race, we must be intentional.

Ethnic groups are outgrowing the white population mainly because of immigration and birthrates. The trend may be new to you, but it is not new to demographers. They have been observing this development for years. And for years I have been telling Christian organizations that they need to prepare, because diversity is coming. That is no longer accurate; diversity is here.

The most common question I receive after imploring people to see color is: "How can I see color and not stereotype?" When I say, "see color," I am talking about a heightened self-awareness. Here are five principles to follow as you see color to keep you from stereotyping.

Humility. Unchecked, racially arrogant attitudes are the quickest way to destructive stereotyping. People tend to frame humility as denigrating self, but that is not what I mean. *Humility* means declining the temptation to put ourselves in God's place. It means following Job's example and figuring out what it means to be submitted before God in his world.

Truth-Telling. With people we truly care about, we're honest about what matters, regardless of how potentially offensive the situation may seem. I contend that for most people, politeness is not the reason they skirt engaging the truth about race. The real reason is they want to protect themselves from conflict. This natural reluctance must be overcome if you and your organization are going to make serious strides. The fear of being uncomfortable is what most hinders reconciliation efforts. But if we refuse to speak the truth because of fear, we are operating as hypocrites. We may be polite hypocrites, but still hypocrites.

Patience. A big reason people don't discuss race is because it can quickly become emotional. It is OK to be emotional, but not in a destructive, all-consuming way. This requires that we work hard to keep our emotions in check. When it comes to racial issues, it takes time to "get it," and no one "gets it" overnight. If we keep this in mind, it will go a long way in helping others realize the significance of racialization. One thing that has helped me is the realization that people can make honest racial mistakes. They really don't know that what they said or did was hurtful. It is possible for someone to do or say something race-influenced but not be a racist. I work hard on giving people the benefit of the doubt, marking them innocent until proven guilty.

Encouragement. Too much time is spent on the negative side of racial dynamics. The term *jaundiced eye* means to approach people with caution. I am contrarian on this. We have to work hard to suspend our root assumptions about people. If we don't, it will lead to stereotyping, which is not good. We need to be careful not to build an atmosphere filled with a constant diatribe on what is wrong while short-changing spending time on what is right or how to move forward. I won't end a conversation about bad racial dynamics until the other party and I have some dialogue about proposed solutions.

Respect. All ethnic groups need to be treated with dignity. One killer of reconciliation efforts is paternalism, the intrusion of one group on another against its will. The intrusion is justified by a claim that the group intruded upon will be "better off." What results is a one-sided relationship.

Discussion Questions

1. How do you classify yourself racially? What criteria did you use to come to your answer?

2. How has your race affected your view of the world? Reflect on how it has shaped your perception of life.

3. How has your race affected your faith? What rituals do you consider to be sacred yet are not based in Scripture but your racial heritage?

4. Have you ever been racially discriminated against, or do you know someone who has? Share the story with the group.

After reading this chapter and going through the discussion questions, what are some topics you and the team should be praying about—personally and organizationally? Share and pray right now.

CHAPTER 3: UNINTENTIONALITY

Summary

When decision-makers are unintentional, people assume there are no problems with ethnic diversity. Most people think that if there is a race problem it's because other people are prejudiced, which of course they feel they are not. Most would agree there were problems in the past with race in the US, but not now.

Extra grace is required when leading. It's hard for people to bring themselves to believe the realities of racialization, and some never will in spite of your best efforts. In their minds, there is not a reality to racism but just *perceived* realities. Racialization is like a bad cold, something people just have to get over. Our response to this type of attitude is critical.

Most organizations don't have multi-ethnicity within their founding DNA, which is the distinguishing doctrine of your particular Christian tradition mixed with the intent of the founder(s) of your particular organization. Whatever the racial practices of the day were, our organizations probably mirrored them. It's your founding DNA which forms the base of your organizational identity.

Like the shift to multiculturalism in the 1970s, we are now in the midst of a paradigm shift into globalization. *Globalization* is a catchall term that describes how foundational social institutions of the world (political, economic, familial, religious, and educational) are moving toward forming global citizens. The challenge at hand is to function together in unity in spite of our differences. Multiculturalism was all about establishing identity, whereas globalization is about existing with mixed identities.

As you move toward intentionality, keep two big cautions in mind. The first is that the days where we can make broad assumptions about people strictly because of their race are gone. As we discussed earlier, race is now just one of many different lenses people use to view the world. Ethnic borders exist all the time, but how important they are is totally based on the individual because of our globalized moment.

Be aware of the rent-a-race mentality, and be wary of zealots, who are not bridge builders any more than those who are "racially rented." Bridge builders are those who have a hybrid personal identity when it comes to ethnicity. It is important for them to understand and stay attached to the ethnic world they represent, while at the same time providing clear understanding to the ethnic others around them.

The second caution is in the area of goal setting. Dr. Larry Crabb stresses mastering the art of differentiating between goals and desires. He defines a goal as "an outcome that requires only my coop-eration to achieve" and a desire as "an outcome that requires the cooperation of another person to be achieved."[3] This is a golden rule that must be followed when leading toward ethnic diversity within your situation. Otherwise, you are setting things up for frustration and anger.

Discussion Questions

1. Are there any historical incidents in your organization where racial issues caused trouble or negative behavior from people? How did the founding DNA help or hurt the situation?

2. Research the racial makeup of both your staff and the constituents you serve. How has your founding DNA contributed to creating this demographic within your organization? Has it helped or hindered it?

3. What are five steps your organization must take in order to move forward? Why have these steps not been taken before now?

4. If these steps are taken, what do you anticipate the reaction will be among your staff and constituents?

5. If you take these next steps what do you lose? What do you gain?

After reading this chapter and going through the discussion questions, what are some topics you and the team should be praying about—personally and organizationally? Share and pray right now.

CHAPTER 4: SUSTAINABLE PERFORMANCE

Summary

I've seen organizations with leaders with good multi-ethnic intentions produce wildly uneven results. I call it the dandelion effect.

An organizational desire arises to either start or advance the process of becoming multi-ethnic. This leads to a frenzy of ideas for multi-ethnic innovation. The will for the management of the programs is driven by vision, collaboration, and innovation. But then the whole process becomes stagnant. The turning point into stagnation is usually marked by a combination of three things: (1) all the "low-hanging fruit" has been picked; (2) enough of the original architects of the vision have left, leaving vision amnesia; or (3) major issues arise that no one has a clear answer for or the will to solve. Diversity efforts then become a flashpoint for organizational politics.

Author Jim Collins in his book *Good to Great* offers the guiding principle: "First who then what." He believes those who build great organizations make sure they have the right people on the bus, the wrong people off the bus, and the right people in the key seats *before* they figure out where to drive the bus. They always think first about who and then about what.[4] Some organizational tasks anybody can do. Such is not the case with ethnic diversity.

It is my observation you will have at least five general camps of worldviews on multi-ethnicity at all times within your organization.

1. Bridge Builders. People in this camp have an innate ability and desire to reconcile racialization, theology, and the founding DNA in very practical ways.

2. Advocates. These are people who demonstrate a strong desire to see their organization be a more ethnically inclusive place, but

they are not as skilled in bridge building. They are important because other camps look to this group for guidance and knowledge about multi-ethnic initiatives.

3. Cautious. This actually may be the most important group, because they link together those who get it early on with those who get it later. Because of their role and the size of the group, they make or break an organization's efforts.

4. Neutralists. These are people who demonstrate a need to not consider the role of race in any particular situation. They will go along to get along, but they won't do so until peer pressure makes it a necessity.

5. Traditionalists. These are people demonstrating a pattern of not being able to discern the practical individual and institutional implications of racialization or the present historical moment.

In light of these five camps, here are a few guidelines for leading:

- Focus on bringing out the best and curtailing the worst.
- Provide as many opportunities as possible for bridge builders and advocates.
- Provide as many resources as possible for the cautious, so they can understand the purpose and need for the changes.
- Provide the same for the neutralists, as they take additional time to consider the changes.
- Provide motivation for the traditionalists. If they hold major decision-making power, they may need to prayerfully consider

moving on, or you may have to lessen their responsibilities so they will not be a roadblock.

The leadership in Acts 6:1–7 modeled how to engage presenting issues. The response was not to be blind to ethnic bias charges, blame the offended ethnic group with causing trouble, or eliminate the concern as the "social gospel." They went to work, and we should follow their lead. I call organizations that display the following traits "Acts 6 organizations." Here are some general characteristics of these types of institutions.

1. They embrace ethnic diversity as an organizational DNA adventure (vv. 1–2). On certain issues, we know every department and organizational stakeholder will be affected. I call those "organizational DNA adventures." We develop long-term plans for things we expect to stick.

2. They leverage ethnic difference (vv. 3–4). It will never be part of the organizational DNA if you cannot thoroughly answer the "why" question. By being consistent in reinforcing the value of ethnic diversity, you will improve the chances of people helping instead of hurting the multi-ethnic change process.

3. They mobilize money and personnel toward solutions (vv. 5–6). If you are going to be serious about multi-ethnicity, it will require a reallocation of resources or focused fund-raising for expansion.

4. They provide clarity (v. 7). Because of the myriad of perspectives brought to the table regarding multi-ethnicity, at times it's difficult to

project a clear vision. So we tend to stay on the surface of this crucial topic, unaware of the assumptions we are making. Unity might be as simple as thoroughly defining the objective.

If we come from a place of strength (assets) we stand a much better chance of moving forward. We must be vigilant to keep the organization in the innovation stage to focus on unearthing assets to utilize toward the multi-ethnic task.

Asset-based diversity development means committing to releasing the capacities and gifts of your employees and the organization. As you do this, you will address the deficiencies and needs. In Acts 6:1–7, the people followed a process of change of being inside out, top down, and all in.

Inside Out. People who work for you have the most to lose and the most to gain. What is needed is an intentional process to unleash the talents of critical stakeholders. Significant diversity development only takes place when those who care most about the organization are committed to bringing it to pass. This is not an either/or decision, to focus internally or bring in outside help; it is a both/and decision. You don't have all the answers within the organization. At times it is strategic to bring in outside voices to hear their perspectives. The more people of color you have who are passionate about your organization and connected to the values of their ethnic community, the better. They will serve as the best catalysts to raise your organizational consciousness about what needs to be done internally.

Top Down. Another variable for sustainable performance is whether major decision-makers embrace or refuse to embrace ethnic diversity. Although the grassroots is important, if anything of significance in this area is going to be accomplished, it will be because the main decision-makers are contributing their time, energy, and resources.

All In. The top of the organizational chart has to drive change, but the grassroots employees play a significant role. Since there are more employees than senior leaders, collectively, they make the final decision whether anything is going to happen. Therefore, it is imperative that we have built-in evaluative systems that surface where people stand on this issue.

Discussion Questions

1. Has your organization experienced the dandelion effect on your multi-ethnic efforts? How can you prevent it in the future?

2. Which of the five camps (bridge builders, advocates, cautious, neutralists, traditionalists) are you in? Explain how you came to your conclusion. Do the people on the team agree?

3. What camp are the major decision-makers in your organization in? Overall, is this a good or bad situation?

4. Would you define yourselves as an Acts 6 organization? Provide the rationale for your answer.

5. To what extent do you agree or disagree with the inside out, top down, all in philosophy?

After reading this chapter and going through the discussion questions, what are some topics you and the team should be praying about—personally and organizationally? Share and pray right now.

CHAPTER 5: MULTI-ETHNIC CHANGE AS SPIRITUAL GROWTH

Summary

By focusing inside out, top down, and all in, the goal is to eventually create a ripple effect. In order to do so, there must be a basic shift from a secular perspective of racial tolerance to a spiritual core of having a strong biblical apologetic, connecting your founding DNA and welcoming the Holy Spirit.

Authors Robert Putnam and David Campbell's research shows that after decades of being the least racially tolerant group (tolerance meaning a permissive racial attitude toward others), evangelicals are now virtually indistinguishable from the rest of the population when it comes to racial attitudes.[5] In today's world, this is a plus because it's the farthest the American church has ever been concerning racial attitudes. But we need to operate very strategically in our globalized historical moment, because although it is a strength, it also has a shadow side.

First, there is the threat of developing a false sense of security. Many believe that racism has ended because of the prevailing atmosphere of racial tolerance. Second, all the celebration of difference, ironically, can create an environment of self-centered ethnocentrism. While the stress is often on gathering information about people's differences, there is no direct correlation between the amounts of information people know and changing moral attitudes. Third, in a supposed "post-racial" world, claims of racial prejudice or discrimination are easily muted. We can't examine power dynamics to determine whose ethnic interests are being served, because we can only see them in positive light in a politically correct atmosphere. Fourth, when something becomes popular, it has a tendency to be taken for granted. When something is taken for granted, it is rarely thought about in a deep way.

The most important point about the shadow side of the age of racial tolerance is that average Christians do not have a practical theology of diversity. What they have at their foundation is racial tolerance. Findings from my personal research are that average Christians:

- think that racial diversity, while important, is not relevant to personal faith;
- think mostly only in terms of black versus white;
- think racial diversity is not critical to the mission of their organizations; and
- are not openly against the concept of racial diversity, but aren't necessarily for it either.

Being Word-based and providing spiritual inspiration are musts for pursuing ethnic diversity. It is the heart of the matter and the core for the asset-based philosophy. It will be the primary incentive for every idea you ask people to implement. If you do not start here, you are leaving the biggest gifts you have—the Bible and your faith—on the sidelines.

If we do not give people biblical motivation for multi-ethnicity, they will probably settle for racial tolerance to fill the void. Racial tolerance is needed for our globalized world to work together, but the church is called beyond tolerance. The Bible calls us to racial transcendence. Our efforts must have the foundation of being Spirit-filled and Word-based. The endgame of our journey of building multi-ethnic institutions is not tolerance; that is a by-product. Give them the motivation to transcend.

The graphic on page 142 illustrates organizational tiers of multi-ethnicity. The first three tiers are either endpoints or phases of development, depending on the situation. Whether you get to the fourth tier is totally dependent on your core and what your main motivation is.

The first tier is segregation, which speaks for itself.

The second tier, assimilation, is what many organizations that claim multi-ethnicity really are. They are multicolored. There may be other ethnic groups present, but their cultural perspective has zero bearing on the opinions, thoughts, or direction of the organization. When you look at the totality of their organizational culture (policies, practices, and procedures), it really only reflects the perspective of the dominating racial group. Those ethnics who stick around are either OK with that setup, or they grin and bear it.

The third tier, toleration, is what our globalized society aims for: tolerance. This is all about getting along. Tolerance is better than assimilation because there are unique and distinctive elements of all races within the organization present in the organizational culture. The organization is mixed-color, indicating progress.

Our desire is to reach the fourth tier: reconciliation. This is where organizational culture is an authentic hybrid of all races represented in the organization. No one dominates the other. Our overarching goal is to have our staffs, boards, faculties, congregants, or students experience deep biblical reflection and practical spiritual application in order for them to grow in their faith. It is a corporate, biblical call of reconciliation, rooted in our faith in God to be able to transcend the troubles of this world that racialization brings.

Acts 6:1–7 is filled with references of the leaders being dependent on the Holy Spirit to guide them in how to solve the presenting issue. Do you have a regular, organized system of prayer for your multi-ethnic desires? I will go so far to say that if the answer is no, then you do not have any right to expect anything to happen. We need to challenge our people to be prayer partners around the change process. We cannot separate who we are spiritually from the task at hand.

Besides being Word-based and Spirit-filled, it is an important asset for decision-makers to tie in the organization's founding DNA in some way to your change efforts. The easiest way to do so is to create a story that ties the valuable traditions of the past with the present multi-ethnic direction of the future. This will personify and give greater worth to the change process you are leading.

Discussion Questions

1. Some people disagree that there is a distinction between racial tolerance and biblical reconciliation. They see racial tolerance as a spiritual, not secular, value. Do you agree or disagree? Why?

2. Looking at the graphic on page 142, what tier is your organization on? What needs to happen to move to the next level?

3. Do you have a practical theology of racial diversity? Does your organization? If not, develop one.

4. Does your organization have an overarching multi-ethnic story tied to the founding DNA? If not, create one.

5. Does your organization have a systematic prayer strategy for the multi-ethnic change process you are undergoing? If not, create one.

After reading this chapter and going through the discussion questions, what are some topics you and the team should be praying about—personally and organizationally? Share and pray right now.

CHAPTER 6: CHANGING THE ETHNIC GAME

Summary

It is much better to initiate change when you can than react to it. Generally speaking, all good leaders are change agents toward vibrant, organizational culture where people can flourish and be all God made them to be. The matter of bold, transformative leadership is big in any change process.

Leading multi-ethnic change is rough, but doable. Don't let the roughness of the terrain fool you into thinking that it is an impossible task. In our base text of Acts 6:1–7, the apostles made direct, administrative changes. They were structured a particular way to meet the needs of the church during a particular season. When that season changed, they were more than willing to adjust.

Structures are designed to serve the season that the organization is in. When seasons change, personnel changes are sometimes necessary. I have never seen a multi-ethnic change process where new structures, policies, practices, procedures, and people were not needed.

The genius of the leaders in Acts 6 was that they were able to make significant organizational changes (vv. 2–6) while keeping the organizational vision fresh and maintaining high morale (v. 7). This is what we are shooting for in the asset-based philosophy and change process. It is our main leadership responsibility.

Tweaking is fear-based change as opposed to Word-based and Spirit-filled. You cannot embark on this journey from the posture of being afraid to rock the boat. Implementing multi-ethnic change is a boat rocker. This is not a cruise ship outing; it's white-water rafting, and you will not be able to tweak your way to success.

We want to lead this process where everybody emerges with their dignities intact. Leading through teams is much more beneficial and way more effective. It will change your organizational culture and make multi-ethnicity a part of the normal way of doing things.

Organizational charts matter. If people at the top don't get it, the rest of the organization will not progress. If you have bridge builders and advocates in a majority of your decision-maker positions, things will take off. If you have a bunch of people from the cautious camp, you will probably go in the right direction but at an incremental, slow pace. If neutralists and traditionalists dominate, good luck!

We all have hills we are willing to die on. You have to decide if multi-ethnicity is one for you. If you don't make it a hill to die on, you will end up doing more harm than good by employing "push hard, then pull back" tactics. The people to whom ethnic diversity matters as well as the bridge builders and advocates will feel betrayed. The cautious, neutralists, and traditionalists will sniff out that you are not truly committed, and they will continue to do the same old thing. It is the quickest way to kill organizational morale.

I define the term *transformational leadership* as getting people to do what they won't naturally do. It is the game changer in the multi-ethnic change process. It is forming and practicing thoughtful, Word-based, Spirit-filled, innovative strategies to bring transformation to the policies, practices, and procedures of your organization that will cause ethnic others to self-select to become a part of your mission. Transformational leadership will be the glue that makes multi-ethnicity stick across the organization. Personally, we are to practice what we preach, and corporately, we are to preach what we practice. This is the heart of multi-ethnic kingdom building.

Every multi-ethnic organizational transformation will have a unique story. With this in mind, let me suggest five transformational components that successful organizations possess for leading toward God's multi-ethnic kingdom. The name of the meal prepared may change, so to speak, but they will all have these ingredients.

1. Major decision-makers are front and center. This is the practical application of a top-down philosophy. Noticeable, vigilant communication from this group exponentially increases the chances of eliminating the dandelion effect.

2. There is either a formal or informal all-in, zero-tolerance policy. Experience has taught me that not involving everyone leaves the impression that organizational diversity initiatives are optional. Make it a part of everyone's job responsibilities in some form or another.

3. They are not the french army. In military circles, the French army is known much more for their ability to tactically retreat than for impressive victories. Don't retreat. Leadership fatigue is a real threat. I've run across many people who have experienced the dandelion effect and decide to give up multi-ethnicity. Keep tackling the hard-hitting presenting issues, since many times the first run will not be successful. But it sets you up well for a second or even third run.

4. They measure success as a value, not simply as numbers. Numbers won't tell the whole story. Remember we are framing multi-ethnicity as spiritual growth. If you move away from this, you may be tempted to implement measures that will build numbers but not cause people to be transformed in their hearts. I know of some organizations that simply buy integration with salaries and benefits packages. They may be multicolored, but they are far from multi-ethnic. And their people are not transformed.

5. They broaden the diversity agenda. Part of being in a post-civil rights era is to avoid isolating race as the only part of personal identity relating to multi-ethnicity. This attitude will come to light when you implement a multi-ethnic change process. People are going to want to know what the plan is for other forms of diversity.

Discussion Questions

1. Are you willing to get fired or resign over the issue of multi-ethnicity? Why or why not?

2. In terms of your views of those ethnically different from you, how have you changed over the years?

3. Describe a successful change experience, either personally or organizationally, that you were a part of. What were the characteristics that made it so successful? How can you apply the lessons learned to the multi-ethnic change process?

4. What will you do differently as a result of reading this chapter?

5. How do you plan on avoiding leadership fatigue in this area?

After reading this chapter and going through the discussion questions, what are some topics you and the team should be praying about—personally and organizationally? Share and pray right now.

CHAPTER 7: PUTTING IT ALL TOGETHER

Summary

In reality you will be working on multiple things at the same time and focusing on some phases more than others, depending on circumstances. As work is being done, it is extremely helpful to keep all your efforts organized and in sync with one another.

A major part of team ministry is alignment, which is constructively positioning people and tasks. Its twin is accountability, which is holding people responsible for an accounting of their activities. Without intentional alignment and accountability, efforts can quickly get sidetracked, misunderstandings can happen, and the door is left wide open for the inertia cycle to start. It also can lead to people doing their own thing in their own way.

In terms of the makeup of the team, make sure you have people with a good reputation, wisdom, and who are filled with the Spirit. Other characteristics of good team members are that they are in sync with organizational theology and philosophy of ministry, are strategic thinkers, and are good relationally.

Alignment and accountability are not measured by whether team members have a good relationship with one another or by spiritual "feel goods" like emotionally encouraging prayer times. They are also not measured by everybody giving good reports on how things are going. These are great team dynamics but not the goal the team should be shooting for. Great team dynamics can actually hurt the process if teams leave their meetings feeling good without actually having accomplished anything. Most likely this type of scenario is because alignment and accountability have been formed around the wrong things. Team identity needs to be formed primarily around workflow.

Strategic planning is the primary purpose of your team. I believe the best way to operate is to develop a rhythm: make a plan, do the plan, check the plan, and adjust to improve the plan. However before you begin planning, there is a major step of clarity that must be taken.

My colleague T. J. Addington uses the illustration of a sandbox to help bring organizational clarity as a whole.[6] He says that there are four areas every organization needs to focus on to maintain its vision. In regards to multi-ethnicity, I maintain that there are four areas of focus to keep your organization in the innovation stage. Playing off of Addington's sandbox, I call it "developing a multi-ethnic picture frame."

The priority is to keep efforts squarely in the innovation stage and out of the inertia stage. The multi-ethnic change process is not something to leave up to chance. Clear expectations must be put in place and accounted for. To invoke alignment and accountability and usher in clarity to the people you lead, there are four basic questions that need to be addressed:

- How does multi-ethnicity tie in to the organizational mission?
- What core commitments need to be made for multi-ethnicity to prosper?
- What will the organization laser-focus on to become more multi-ethnic?
- What type of environment needs to exist for the value of multi-ethnicity to thrive?

Think of these as the four sides of your multi-ethnic picture frame: mission, core commitments, laser-focus, and environment.

Once all these sides have been made clear, the challenge for the team is to align and stay accountable so that everybody is working on painting the same multi-ethnic picture. Once the picture is painted, clear roles for specific people can be developed through accountability action plans.

Mission. Having a mission statement with an overt declaration toward multi-ethnicity would be ideal. However, I understand that mission statements in some places are sacred cows, never to be altered. If you can't change the mission statement, work with it until you understand how you can tie it to your diversity efforts.

Core Commitments. Core commitments are the equivalent to giving people the rules and strategy of the game. People need guiding principles that the organization is committed to following in your multi-ethnic efforts. These commitments define the rules of operation and should be measurable. They are the behavioral guidelines.

Laser Focus. By laser focus I mean figuring out what is the primary thing that must be done every day for your organization to progress multi-ethnically. It is the serious action that will bring the maximum results. Taking into consideration your mission, it is the one thing that you must focus on with a laser-like intensity.

Environment. When it comes to multi-ethnicity, environment is huge. You can have all the other sides of the frame built, but if this one does not come together, it doesn't matter what you do in the others. An environment must be created for the ethnic other to prosper.

Discussion Questions

1. Who will serve on the implementation team? Ideally someone from senior leadership who is a bridge builder or advocate will serve as leader. Create your team.

2. As a training exercise, read the case study in the next section and work through the questions provided. What did you discover?

3. What will your organization's mulit-ethnic picture frame look like? As a team, create it. This will serve as your highest form of clarity.

4. What will be your first issue to tackle? As a team, begin the cycle of plan, do, check, and adjust.

After reading this chapter and going through the discussion questions, what are some topics you and the team should be praying about—personally and organizationally? Share and pray right now.

NOTES

1. Michael O. Emerson and Christian Smith, *Divided by Faith: Evangelical Religion and the Problem of Race in America* (Oxford: Oxford University Press, 2000), 7.

2. Andrew Walls, *The Missionary Movement in Christian History: Studies in the Transmission of Faith* (Maryknoll, N.Y.: Orbis, 1996), 53.

3. Larry Crabb, *How to Deal with Anger* (Grand Rapids, Mich.: Zondervan, 1982), 8–12.

4. Jim Collins, *Good to Great: Why Some Companies Make the Leap . . . and Others Don't* (New York: HarperCollins, 2001), 41.

5. Robert D. Putnam and David E. Campbell, *American Grace: How Religion Divides and Unites Us* (New York: Simon & Schuster, 2010).

6. T. J. Addington, *Leading from the Sandbox: How to Develop, Empower, and Release High-Impact Ministry Teams* (Colorado Springs: NavPress, 2010).

CASE STUDY

This section will give you an opportunity to actively apply what you have read in the text.

MARSHA AND HEATH

Case studies provide excellent opportunities for learning. Before delving into the "real world" of your organization, it would be great for you and your team to tackle the fictional issues of Marsha and Heath. They are fictional only in the sense that I have changed names and scenarios, but they are real in the fact that they are a compilation of issues I have run across in over twenty years of practice and consultations.

❧

Marsha grew up in the well-to-do suburb of Indian Hill, northeast of Cincinnati. She's always been great at academics, demonstrated by the bachelor and master's degrees in education she earned at University of Cincinnati in a five-year period.

Heath is from Hicksville, a sleepy town three hours from Cincinnati near the Ohio/Indiana border where he spent his childhood. Following in the footsteps of his father, he attended Cincinnati Christian University to study for the pastorate. Marsha and Heath first met as college seniors while they served as tutors at an inner-city elementary school. It was love at first sight, and after graduation, they married.

For the first few years of their careers, both of them bounced around the Cincinnati metro area—Heath as a youth pastor and Marsha as a teacher. Last year they found gold both personally and professionally. Marsha moved from the classroom to administration by becoming principal of North College Hill Christian Academy. At the same time, Heath took on the senior pastorate of River City Church, a mere five minutes from Marsha's school.

Naturally, after landing jobs in the same community, they became intrigued by the idea of buying a house in North College Hill. They quickly found a modest three-bedroom, moved in, and began bonding with their neighbors. But that was last year. Now, they are wondering what in the world they have gotten themselves into. The boards of both the church and school have raised questions about what to do about the demographic shift taking place in North College Hill.

The fact is that for the first time in their lives, as whites, Marsha and Heath are the minorities on their street. At most of the restaurants, gas stations, and other service industries in the neighborhood, the workers seem to be immigrants. A few low-income apartment complexes have even sprung up nearby. These trends really don't bother them. Both Heath and Marsha have been proactive in addressing these trends, beginning by changing the organizational leadership at the church and the Christian school.

For the first time in the history of Heath's predominately white church, he led the way for an African-American elder (Don) to be appointed. Marsha recruited both a businesswoman of Puerto Rican descent (Maria) and one of her former classmates (David), a second-generation Asian-American, to serve on the school board.

Heath and Marsha were not prepared, though, for some of the actions and attitudes of their fellow Christians in the face of these demographic changes. The predominant responses were negative, based on fear. "I'm getting out while I can, while my house still has value," one of the church's former elders privately told Heath as he moved to another neighborhood. Heath has also had to deal with a divided elder board concerning one of the ministry programs of Barry, the youth pastor.

On Sunday nights, Barry plays basketball to build relationships with students. The group that shows up is becoming more and more racially diverse as the neighborhood changes, with fewer youth coming from families in the predominantly white church. Barry has really connected with a substantial group of both low-income and nonwhite youth through this outreach. This demographic change in who frequents the building is worrying some church members.

At Marsha's school, parents are threatening to take their kids out if the school decides to "urbanize." Joe, a well-respected teacher, has already left to work at another school. He cited that he did not sign up to teach "those type of kids" when the board held a controversial vote over a proposal to create a racial diversity scholarship fund.

What is most perplexing to Heath and Marsha is that these people who are, in their opinion, acting so callously seem to be people of strong character, good intentions, and solid biblical beliefs. The elders who are so upset about the racially different kids coming to open gym are the same ones who wanted a gym built onto the church for a sports outreach ministry! And doesn't Joe weekly volunteer in a poverty-stricken part of Cincinnati to tutor kids? To Heath and Marsha, it just doesn't make sense.

Heath calls an emergency elder-board meeting. He can feel the tension in the room. "We all know why we are here," he begins. "I want to discuss the firestorm that is brewing over Barry's open-gym policy. It seems that it has caused some people in the church to be uncomfortable." Various elders begin speaking up.

"I don't know why," Greg says. "I was against building the gym in the first place for financial reasons, but now that I see it is bringing in unsaved kids from the neighborhood and exposing them to our ministry, I'm all for it. Isn't that what we wanted?"

"Well, yeah," Don says, "but not *all* kids. I mean, we don't want the thug element coming in and causing trouble. I went for a couple of minutes last week to see how things were going, and it looked like a hip-hop video in there! No wonder my son doesn't want to come to open gym anymore."

The elders are shocked. They were sure that an African-American would be all for keeping the open-gym policy. Heath swallows hard and asks the elephant-in-the-room question. "Don, I'm not trying to be racist or disrespectful, but I'm surprised to hear that comment from you. I thought you would be pleased that open gym is drawing a lot of African-American and Latino kids."

"No offense taken, Pastor," Don replies. "Let me explain. My wife and I grew up downtown. When my wife became pregnant, we decided that we did not want to raise our children around the same negative influences we had to cope with. So we moved to North College Hill. Now I think we might have to move out farther, maybe West Chester. But we're committed to the church. We want our kids to go to a good school, have a nice big house, and basically experience a better quality of life. I did not go to grad school and I do not work sixty-hour weeks so that my son can hang around kids like that."

"Kids like what?" Greg asks.

"Kids who are bad influences."

"How do you know they are bad influences?" Greg continues. "Have you met any of them?"

"No. But I don't have to. I grew up around them, so I know what they are about."

"I think you're unfairly labeling them as thugs," Greg gently pushes. "As far as I know, there has not been one incident of anything bad happening at open gym. In fact, my son has become good friends with Rico who found out about our church through coming to open gym and now comes to the student small groups on his own! He takes the bus. I've had him over for dinner, and he seems like a solid young man—the furthest thing from a thug."

Silence fills the room as Don continues to stir.

"Well, I agree with Don," Chris says. "I mean, we all know we are to love our neighbors and be accepting of others, and we do that.

I think we are a color-blind church. We have Don on our board, don't we? Rico may be OK, but what about the others? We need some sort of policy to govern this type of thing."

"That's ridiculous!" Greg exclaims. "Are you seriously suggesting that we select the types of kids we allow to come to open gym?"

"Something like that," Chris replies matter-of-factly.

"That's the most ridiculous thing I've ever heard!" Greg says.

"It's not ridiculous at all," Don adds. "It's protecting our investment and the quality of our ministry."

"This is going to be a long night," Heath thinks to himself.

◦◦◦

This is the meeting Marsha did not want to facilitate. Last month, a heated debate took place between board members over whether to establish a scholarship program to increase both racial and economic diversity at the school. Marsha saw this fund as a tool to address the developing demographic trends of the region. Although the community is racially changing, the school remains 98 percent white and 100 percent upper middle class. The vote last month was seven to five to establish the racial diversity fund and has caused a stir among the teachers, staff, and parents.

"Let's try to bring closure to the scholarship-fund debate," Marsha states. "It seems to have caused quite a fuss, and I don't know why."

"I'll tell you why," Maria responds. "It's because this place is filled with racists and yuppies. Only in a backward place like Cincinnati would people not want racial and economic diversity!"

"Whoa, hold on. Why do we need such diversity?" asks Phil, elder statesman of the board. Phil's family was part of the first twenty families who enrolled students in the school when it opened in 1970. He is also the school's largest donor. These two factors make him the most influential member of the board. "This is the United States of America!" he continues. "I didn't want the diversity fund because those people are loafers. It's bad enough my tax dollars are going to them. I definitely don't want my donations contributing to their sin. Quite frankly Marsha, if I had known you wanted those types of students in this school, we never would have hired you in the first place."

Marsha is dumbfounded by Phil's comment. Before she can respond, an equally exasperated Maria chimes back in.

"Sin? What have they done?" Maria asks.

"Well, for starters, the poor ones won't go to work," Phil fires back. "The Bible says if a man won't work he shouldn't eat. We all know they are on the government dole. I didn't come from money. My parents did what they had to do for the family to make it. We didn't get one red cent from welfare programs. Why can't they do the same? They've got to learn to pull themselves up by their own bootstraps. And why should race be tied into who gets financial help?

We're Christians. I mean, when I see a black man, all I see is a man. I don't see color. Besides, it might also open the door for us letting in illegal immigrant kids, and then we have an ethical issue to deal with because we are supporting lawbreakers."

"Grandpa, chill!" Mike interrupts. "I mean, who even talks like that anymore?" Mike is an architect, the newest member of the board, and Phil's twenty-five-year-old grandson. "This fund is needed to give us both ethnic and economic diversity," he continues. "Have you looked at the neighborhood lately? Better yet, have you looked at the world? We are doing our students a disservice if we don't bring the real world into the building."

"David," Marsha interjects, mainly to call a halt to the generational family feud, "do you have an opinion? I really would like to hear your perspective."

"Research shows that most students and families of low income, if given the proper help, achieve at the same rate as students in other social classes," David replies. "So I voted for the fund to offer that help."

"Look," Phil adds, "I am just expressing good old-fashioned biblical values. I'm not condemning them. I just expect more from them. I repeat—this is America, where we can all make it with good hard work. And how can we be operating as Christians if we inadvertently support a Democratic platform like racial diversity and illegal immigration, which we will with this fund? Marsha and Maria, I know you are women and want to mother everybody, but you two are going too far. You've got to think like men on this; kids nowadays need tough love, not handouts."

Maria and Martha look at each other and roll their eyes.

"Phil would you please refrain from making assumptions based on gender? Let's focus on the real issues here," Marsha replies.

"We're not talking about handouts with this fund, but a hand up," Maria argues. "Phil, I'll tell you what: There were many, many times that if my family didn't get help from the government, I would not have eaten. Offering them help with their education is the least we can do. That's why I voted for it. You can't make it in this country without an education. Combine that with the gospel, and that's the best hand up you can give somebody."

"Well, this school will be looking for a hand up soon." Phil says. "Our best teacher has left, and I'm sure others will follow. At the last parent meeting, we almost had a mutiny on our hands. I've been told there are major donors who are going to demand we shut down the racial diversity fund or they will pull out their money, which is going to hurt us big-time financially. What are you going to do about this?"

Everyone's eyes immediately turn to Marsha.

Heath heads up the interstate to Hicksville to spend the day with his father, Chuck. His dad has always been his biggest source of wisdom about not only ministry, but life in general. After exchanging pleasantries over lunch and hearing about the elder meeting, Chuck offers some advice.

"Son, to tell you the truth, I don't know if you have a solvable problem."

"That can't be true, Dad. I mean, they make it work in the secular world right? They deal with racial issues all the time."

"It's different for them," Chuck replies. "They have laws they have to follow, and money is tied to integration and things like that. You run a church. In a church, people only do things if they want to. The only power you have is influence."

"Isn't the gospel supposed to solve all problems?" Heath asks. "In college they emphasized how the world is coming to our borders, and stressed how people need to be united by faith. And then during that six-month internship I did at a multi-ethnic urban church, I matured in my faith so rapidly. Why can't I make it work now?"

"That was the pie-in-the-sky world of Christian college," Chuck reminds his son. "This is real life. And Don had a point: You and Marsha loved living downtown when you were first married, but when you were expecting your first child, you turned down the offer to become pastor of an urban church because of the same issues Don raised."

Heath feels his stomach churn as his dad continues.

"Your ministry was doing fine until this open-gym controversy came up. I don't know what to tell you, because I don't have to deal with that type of stuff out here."

"Not yet," Heath answers. "There's that group of businessmen who want to bring in the meat-packing plant. Latino families will come here in droves if that happens."

"Look, Heath, it's just different out here." They're both silent for a few long moments. Then Chuck speaks up, "You know, now that I think about it, I may have an answer to your problem."

"I'm listening," Heath replies.

"Well, I told my elder board two weeks ago that I'll be ready to retire soon. Thirty years in the ministry is long enough. The first thing they asked was if you would be willing to come home to take over. I told them no, but that was before I knew about this situation. Heath, it's only going to get worse concerning this racial stuff. Maybe you ought to come back to Hicksville."

"What about Marsha? She loves her job."

"Well, you know that the high school principal is a member of my church. I overheard him say the other day he will be looking for a new assistant principal. I could investigate if you want."

"I don't know what I want, Dad. I just don't know."

❧

As she drives home from the board meeting, Marsha has the biggest headache ever. Both sides seem to have good points. Maria is right: Christians are supposed to help the poor. But she knows that Phil is right too: Joe leaving was a major blow, and if some major donors leave, it will cause major financial hardship. This also has the potential to create a major perception problem in the community.

Marsha is leaning toward being financially pragmatic about the whole matter. She could take the proposal off the table and reason that the school isn't ready for a move like this. That would make the whole thing go away for the most part, and she would just have to smooth things over with a couple of board members. But at least the budget would be balanced.

But she can't convince herself that this is the biblical thing to do. After all, the majority of the board feels that the time is right, regardless of the financial consequences. Marsha also feels guilty. She drove her parents crazy because she refused to go to Christian, rural Cedarville University herself as a student. With missionary zeal, she went to University of Cincinnati in order to take her faith to the "real world."

She remembers all of the racially diverse friendships she made while there and the time she led her Muslim roommate to the Lord. She remembers the volunteering she did in the poorer areas of Cincinnati through the Christian campus group. She also remembers how she and Heath bought an old, rundown duplex early in their marriage and rehabbed it to help change the community. But everything changed when she became pregnant.

When Heath had to choose between pastorates, they chose the one in North College Hill, because they felt that would be the most comfortable family life. Before pregnancy she was gung ho about tackling racial diversity, but when push came to shove she wanted to be comfortable. Now, she feels privileged and guilty that she even had the choice to lead a more comfortable life.

In fact, this controversy has made her realize that guilt was what drove her to embrace racial diversity in the first place—the guilt she felt for growing up white and upper middle class in a society that she feels favors her. She believes that people of color and low income are treated unjustly in this country and she wants to make restitution. "But why should I feel guilty?" she thinks.

She doesn't use any racial slurs and supports immigration reform. She's respectful to people of other ethnicities and social classes and will raise her children to be as well. Maybe she should just realize that she can't save the world, but she can save the school. The more she thinks, the worse her headache becomes.

DISCUSSION STARTERS

1. As a team, identify the challenges of ethnic borders, racialization, and unintentionality in Marsha's and Heath's situations.

2. As a team, based on what you have read in chapters 4–7, take the role of Heath and Marsha and write a strategic plan for their presenting issues.

SERVICES AVAILABLE

Alvin works with many churches, Christian universities, and nonprofit organizations concerning the issues outlined in this book. Services available include plenary speaking, seminars or workshops, and consultations. If you are interested in Alvin's availability and ministry, contact him at:

E-mail: alvin.sanders87@gmail.com

Twitter: AlvinSanders1

Blog: http://alvinsanders.net